THE POCKET GUIDE TO
Manifesting

BY MEGAN BORD

Edited by Chris W. Malcomb

For ~ A ~

Thanks for believing in me
And being my forever friend

The Pocket Guide to Manifesting

COPYRIGHT © 2013 by Megan Bord

All rights reserved. No part of this book may be used or reproduced in any manner without written permission of the author except in the case of brief quotations embodied in critical articles or reviews.

Cover artwork by Mary Beth Dolan, Copyright 2013, all rights reserved.

CONTENTS

INTRODUCTION	1
PART ONE: What *Is* Manifesting?	9
PART TWO: The Four Main Steps	13
STEP ONE: Establish A Positive Foundation	13
Positive Attracts Positive	13
Keep An Open Mind	15
Lighten Up!	16
STEP TWO: State What You Want	17
But What Do You Really, REALLY Want?	19
Specific or Loose?	22
STEP THREE: Feel As If You Already Have Whatever It Is You Want	25
Hold On To That Feeling!	31
STEP FOUR: Let the Universe Figure Out Delivery Options	37
PART THREE: The Roles of Visualization & Affirmation	41
PART FOUR: Additional Tools & Helpful Hints	55
PART FIVE: Q & A	76
PART SIX: Living Life to Its Fullest	90
APPENDIX 1: More Real Life Examples	92
APPENDIX 2: My Manifestation Worksheet	110

INTRODUCTION

I remember once having this thought: "It'd be cool to date a pilot." A few days later, when I opened my email inbox, I had a new message from a man on an online dating site I'd joined who wanted get to know me better. We exchanged a few pleasant emails before I asked him how he earned his living. "I'm a pilot," he wrote. "I fly commercial and private airplanes." You think I would have been shocked by his response, but I wasn't. See, that's just how things go: I think the thought, and then effortlessly, *my thoughts turn into real stuff*. Like magic.

Sound cool? Well, here's another one: I know two great guys who own a bakery and sell at farmers' markets and arts festivals. One day an idea popped into my head: "It'd be fun to work for those guys sometime." The next week when I saw them at my local market, the owner pulled me aside and said, unsolicited, "We'd like you to work for us at an upcoming festival this year. What do you think? Will you do it?!" My reply was an emphatic YES!

How could this baker have known what was in my head without me telling him? How could the pilot who contacted me out of the blue have known that I'd recently wished to date a pilot? What is happening when mental ideas and images suddenly become reality? And, more importantly, have you ever wished this could happen to *you*?

I grew up watching TV shows like *Bewitched* and *I Dream Of Jeannie*, pretending that through the blink of my eyes or by snapping my fingers, I could make stuff appear out of thin air. There was something absolutely alluring about magic – the possibilities of a world beyond what my eyes could see, the idea that I could be, do or *have* anything I wanted. I desperately wanted to have powers like Samantha and Jeannie, even though my conscious mind was certain that it was all just make believe.

It wasn't until my late 20's or early 30's that I stumbled onto the idea of manifesting and started discovering, more and more, that I actually *could* use my thoughts to create something out of nothing. I remember the first time I watched the movie *The Secret* and heard author and manifesting master Mike Dooley utter the phrase, "Thoughts become things." To the uninitiated, that phrase might seem too simple, maybe even evoking a response like, "Duh!" After all, *any* thought can become a thing if someone has the wherewithal to act upon it and bring it to fruition. But to me, and to anyone who lives in the magical world of manifesting, I've learned that we don't need a complicated master plan, elbow grease, or other "nose to the grindstone" effort to get there. In fact, the truth is that, in no uncertain terms, ***what we think about we bring about.***

So how did I get to be good at manifesting? Well, first, let me share that it wasn't always this way. From a material standpoint I came from a modest upbringing: my parents divorced when I was eleven, and whatever money we had before that point left with my father. Times were tight throughout my teenage years, too, so my attitude toward life was best summed up as, "You've got to work (hard) for what you want."

And work I did! Starting at a young age, I babysat, cleaned houses and hair salons, and took on many other odd jobs to earn money. While these were great experiences, I've since learned that I actually don't want to work *that hard* just for stuff. What's more, I don't really *ever* want to "work," at least in the traditional sense of the word. I want to enjoy my life and spend time doing what I want, with whom I want, when I want!

My parents' divorce also greatly impacted myself-esteem. While I appeared confident on the outside, inside I was always scared of not being good enough. Worse yet, I was terrified that others would discover this flaw. As a result, I pushed myself to the point of perfection in all facets of life. At school, I worked obsessively to earn straight

A's. At home, I tried to be the perfect kid by cooking, cleaning, minding my manners, and taking care of other people's needs. As a young woman, I took up exercise and studied nutrition to mold my body into the images I saw in the mass media. All of my efforts were attempts to compensate for who I actually was; to try and fix the "broken" parts of myself I thought no one could love, not even me.

So, why am I telling you all of this? Well, mostly to let you know that despite a challenging early life and misguided beliefs about myself, *discovering manifesting helped me overcome every obstacle.* Had I grown up as a rich girl who was given everything she ever wanted, I might not feel myself to be as credible at manifesting as I currently do. Am I an expert? No way! Truthfully, I wouldn't consider myself an "expert" at anything, but I've had enough success with manifesting to know that I'm darn good at it! The bottom line is that I'm an ordinary person who figured out how to use thoughts and feelings to attract extraordinary experiences in miraculous ways. Simply ask those who know me. They're the ones who prodded me to write this book.

The Pocket Guide to Manifesting

By now you're probably craving some hard evidence, proof that, under the right conditions, thoughts *really do* become things. OK, then! I'll start with some of my best manifesting experiences to-date:

» **WEALTH.** I was once offered a $900,000 per year job, for which I had never interviewed, four hours after having the thought, "I wonder what it would be like to be a millionaire?"

» **JOB.** During an interview for a promotion, which would place me in a prominent position within the company I worked for at the time, I manifested being offered the job on-the-spot. That happened just eight hours after I envisioned how I wanted the interview to go. On top of that, the next morning I manifested a 60% pay raise after they only initially wanted to give me 10% for the promotion.

» **TRAVEL.** One time I thought, "It'd be cool to go to Scotland." A few months later and not having shared my thoughts aloud, a friend suggested we take a trip overseas. He offered to pay, and let me choose the location. Scotland anyone?!

» **ROMANCE.** Never one to sleep around and without so much as a warm lead, I once manifested the most passionate, sensual, romantic weekend I'd yet had with a "perfect for me" guy. Who was he? Someone I met four years prior and on whom I'd had a crush the moment our eyes met. Trouble was, he lived on the opposite US coast from me and during those four years we hadn't kept in good touch. Enter manifesting, which resulted in a blissful, mind-blowing weekend that happened effortlessly.

» **CAREER CHANGE.** After taking a one-year sabbatical from the corporate world, I wanted to start working again, but on my terms: from home, part-time with full-time pay, benefits, with and for someone I respected. Oh, and I wanted to do something fun, easy and fulfilling. What did I end up with? A veritable dream job working as a personal assistant to a millionaire. The details of which included part-time hours with full-time pay, benefits, working from home, doing fun and easy tasks and working for and with someone I respected.

I'm telling you, this stuff is easy, is a blast and is open to anyone! So let's get to it, already! Before we begin, though, a tiny bit of housekeeping. When I started writing this book, I envisioned who my "ideal" reader would be. Of course *anyone* can benefit from reading it, but I think this guide is particularly well-suited for people who:

» Are familiar with the "law of attraction," but still struggle with it somehow (like getting it to function the way they want it to more times than not)

- » Are open-minded and optimistic
- » Want to "hit the ground running" and get straight to manifesting without spending a whole lot of time learning how or why it works

Contrarily, this book probably isn't a good fit for pessimists or people who are convinced *they have to work hard* to get anything good in life. As I said before, I'm all about keeping things simple and easy. Oh, and since I'm not calling myself an expert, I won't go into detailed explanations of what manifesting is or why it works. If the "nuts-and-bolts" scientific and/or metaphysical perspectives interest you, there are plenty of great books you can reference. As for me, I'll avoid the complicated stuff and just share what makes sense to me and matches my own experiences. Sound good? OK, then, *now* let's get started!

Everything is possible.

Believe in *magic*.

PART ONE: What *Is* Manifesting?

While most dictionaries define manifesting as "making clear or evident to the eye," I'd say it more like this: *manifesting is the art of creating something out of nothing.* True manifesting goes beyond, let's say, making a pizza from scratch when you already have the ingredients on-hand and just decide you're hungry for pizza. Instead, it's about simply thinking "Boy, it sure would be nice to have pizza right now" when you don't have any pizza ingredients and haven't phoned in an order, and having a delivery person ring your doorbell a half-hour later with a pizza they swear is for you...and already paid for! *That's* my kind of manifesting!

Let's go back to the example of manifesting a $900,000 per year job four hours after having the thought, "I wonder what it would be like to be a millionaire?" I didn't tell anyone about my desire to be a millionaire. Actually, I was in the shower when I was working that particular bit of manifesting magic. Somewhere between shampooing my hair and soaping my body, I took 30 seconds to imagine the feeling of being really, really rich. And when I say I could *feel* myself as a millionaire, I mean that I was able to – for maybe a split second or two – absolutely *know* what it was like to easily purchase anything I wanted. For those couple of moments,

I wasn't thinking about being a millionaire, I actually *was* a millionaire from shampooed head to soapy toes.

After my shower, I sort of forgot about it and went back into "regular person" mode. I happened to be flying to Florida to visit my mother that day, and it was during my layover, in fact, that I received an unexpected email from a former coworker. In it he explained that he had told a well-to-do overseas company about me, and, based on his favorable description and subsequent recommendation, they wanted to hire me on-the-spot for $900,000 a year, plus bonus. Now, the really cool thing is that this friend had no way of knowing that four hours earlier I'd been in the shower manifesting millionaire status, nor did I know that he was linked up with such a wealthy, generous company! And yet that's just how manifesting works: *it makes something clear or evident to the eye that previously was just a thought or feeling.*

Skeptics might chalk my last example up to coincidence. They're free to do that, of course, but I should state that I really don't believe in coincidence, or at least not in the traditional sense. Coincidence implies "chance," and that's not how I've come to understand my personal experience of manifesting. Instead, I believe that as thinking/feeling human beings, we *draw* every experience to us as if we're magnetic.

Manifesting works on the premise that every person, place, and thing in life is comprised of energy. What's more, this energy vibrates at different frequencies, each of which are attracted to one another based on their similarities. This is the "Like attracts like" principle in action at its most essential level.

As humans, not only are we comprised of energy, but *our thoughts and emotions are also energetic.* Each of our thoughts travels out into the world and draws toward us experiences that match in frequency. In other words, we draw to us the very experiences we think about! Emotions come into play by fine-tuning the frequency of our thoughts and speeding up how quickly we're attracting whatever it is we're focused on.

How Emotions Speed Up Manifesting

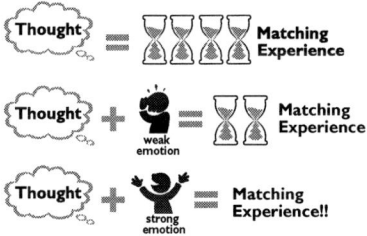

Going back to the $900,000 job offer, I believe the fact that I could *feel* what it would be like to be really, really rich is what attracted the offer to me that day. Was it the first time

I thought about being a millionaire? No. It had probably been in my mental coffers for quite some time. Like many of us, I'd surely spent a great deal of time dreaming of winning the lottery and living a life of ease and luxury. However, I hadn't – before that day – fully *felt* what it would be like to have such abundant wealth. Adding strong emotion to my thoughts was the missing magical ingredient that drew the offer to me in record time. In fact, feeling has, time and again, proven to be the linchpin in anything I've tried to manifest.

Speaking of process, let's cut to the chase and talk about how to start manifesting more effectively.

PART TWO:
The Four Main Steps

If I wanted to keep things really easy and fun, I could sum up how to manifest with this: "Envision the end result you're after and feel what it would be like if it was yours *right now*. Then just sit back watch it happen." BAM! Done. That might be a tad too simplistic for a guide, though, so I'll offer a *bit* more detail. In this section I'll talk about the four major steps in the manifesting process:

1. Establish a Positive Foundation
2. State What You Want
3. FEEL As If You Already Have What You Want
4. Let the Universe Figure Out Delivery Options

STEP ONE:
Establish a Positive Foundation

Positive Attracts Positive

In the previous section we discussed that every thought we think affects our future by acting as a magnet. With this in mind, it makes sense that we would then need to maintain a certain mindset if we wanted to draw truly magical experiences to us. Not unlike exercising a body to keep it in great physical shape, we have to mold our minds into *purely positive* machines so that we manifest only positive end results. The operative words here are purely positive, since it's just as easy to magnetize *negative* experiences to us. If you're like me, however, you'd prefer to err on the side of positivity!

It's important to remember that *we're always manifesting something*. Manifesting doesn't start the moment we consciously state, "I'm going to start manifesting now." It's *always* happening because we're *always* thinking and *always* feeling. So if you were to look around at your life right now, could you size up – by the people, things and experiences around you – what your general mindset is? Are you struggling in life at all or do you see a lot of negativity around you? If so, you could likely use some positive mental reconditioning. On the other hand, if you're fairly content with how your life is but just want to embellish it a bit, you probably have a fairly positive mindset working.

I was a pretty negative person in my early 20's. I was sarcastic, cynical, and felt like a victim most of the time. What's more, I was insecure, thinking that whatever I had could be taken away at any moment, including the affection of friends, lovers, and family. Heck, I may even have been a bit paranoid! As a result, the experiences that showed up in my life matched my mindset: my car was broken into; I was nearly thrown out of my apartment; my longtime boyfriend cheated on me; I had health issues, lived paycheck-to-paycheck, and hated my job. In addition, I witnessed a lot of arguments and engaged in some pretty nasty ones myself! In short, I was a "negativity magnet."

Then one day I decided to turn my mindset around. I began reading books on becoming a more positive person and started policing my thoughts for negativity, instantly replacing negative thoughts with positive ones. I limited the negative influences in my life, as well. I stopped watching, reading or listening to the news and eventually gave away my television. I stopped reading gossip magazines and finally began to withdraw from negative conversations and people.

As I began weeding out negative and replacing it with positive, my life started to look a lot different to me. I started naturally attracting more positive people and experiences. I landed a job I enjoyed and was given promotions and raises effortlessly, which meant no longer living paycheck-to-paycheck. My health greatly improved and I laughed more and smiled more easily. I stopped overhearing gossip, arguments, or witnessing other tense moments, and everyone around me seemed to like their life as much as I did!

So essentially what I'm saying is that positive thinking helps attract positive experiences, and it's something you can condition your mind to do on a regular basis.

Keep An Open Mind

Another thing we have to do when we're consciously manifesting is expand our mind to allow for the idea that *everything is truly possible*. We live in an unlimited

Universe where if we can *think* it, we can *have* it. So try it right now: soften your mind and let go of all the things you think you know, because magic defies logic. In Zen practice, a "beginner's mind" is used to describe this open, curious place that remains uninfluenced by past conditioning from ideas or experiences. So as you soften, try to remain as "beginner" as you can, staying open to the idea that the Universe *wants* to surprise and delight you, that it *wants* to deliver you miracles, and your deepest wishes, if you can find a way to allow your mind – your thoughts – to welcome all of that goodness in.

Lighten Up!

In this brick-and-mortar world, we aren't often granted opportunities to let loose and give our imaginations free reign. But manifesting is fun, so rather than thinking about it as another task to accomplish, try and see it as playtime. The Universe exists to *fulfill* everyone's desires, not deny them, so take advantage and understand, dream big and get wild! Imagine for yourself the greatest things ever and know that because there is an energetic interconnectedness between all people and things, the things you want *also want you.*

Try this right now: Take a minute to envisage that life looks like a big field of bubbles where every conceivable experience involving a person, place or thing is floating around in endless supply, waiting for a corresponding human thought/feeling to call it in. Now imagine that you, too, are a bubble floating in the same field, and each thought/feeling you have starts to draw other "like energy" bubbles your way. The more often you have a particular thought/feeling, or the stronger that thought/feeling is, the faster your bubbles are drawn together. What's the only limitation to manifesting? Our minds and *how big we let ourselves dream.*

STEP TWO:
State What You Want

Once you have a positive mental foundation laid, you're ready to get clear and state specifically what it is you want. Here's where you write it down, say it aloud, think it in your head, draw it or clarify it in whatever form works best for you.

Years ago, when I wanted to manifest a new group of friends, I went a step beyond imagining myself surrounded by a bunch of new people, laughing and having a great time. That was a fine start, but my brain tends to need more focus than that. So instead I created a word collage that I hung on my kitchen cupboard and looked at every day until a new group of friends began to develop. In big, bold print I put the words "MY FRIENDS," beneath which I put an array of adjectives like "open minded," "fun," "happy," "numerous," "smart" and "varied."

Once I had established the basic characteristics of my new group of friends, I thought about *why* I wanted to manifest them to begin with. This led to an even more focused group of adjectives. At the time, I had many wonderful friends but several lived far away, and the ones who didn't weren't always available to hang out or talk. This left me feeling alone much of the time. So I decided to add the following words to the collage: "close-by," "always available to me" and "we enjoy spending time together." Then for good measure I threw in "supportive" and "always make me feel special" (because who doesn't want to feel special?!).

By the time I was done, I had a clear and easily envisioned list of what I wanted from a new group of friends. What's more, because I took thirty seconds each day to look at the words in my collage, I soon began to notice changes in my existing friendships and went from spending the majority of my time alone to spending at least half my time with good company.

Now, writing it down isn't the only way to do it. As I mentioned before, it doesn't really matter what means you use to state your desires. What *is* important is that you state them clearly – as much for yourself as for the Universe when it does your bidding.

But What Do You Really, REALLY Want?

OK, I know you may be thinking, "We just covered this part!" Well, we have. But here's an important addendum. Once you think you've gotten clear about what it is you want, you need to get *even clearer* and decide what it is you really, REALLY want.

Yep, two "reallys," and here's why: *the Universe wants to give us **whatever** we ask for.* It absolutely does! And not only that, but it wants to do it in the quickest, best way possible. You may be thinking, "Great! So why doesn't it?" Well, something pretty big gets in the way. Humans. Yes, we get in our own way! With these beautiful brains of ours, we often think (without thinking) that we already know how something might happen, but we're not always *aware* that's what we're doing.

Take this example. One summer, I wanted to see Ray Lamontagne in concert when he came to my hometown. At the time I loved him and his music. I must have listened to "Beg, Steal or Borrow" one hundred times if I listened to it once, and I couldn't hear the opening notes of "For the Summer" without turning up the volume and letting loose, karaoke-style, in my car. I decided, however, that rather than pay for tickets to the concert, I'd win them from a local radio show. For three weeks, I called into the show whenever they announced the lines were open. Despite my optimism, lightning fast fingers and tenacity, I came up short. So I began to question my manifesting abilities. What was I doing wrong? I'd envisioned myself acting surprised and thanking the radio host when he told me I was the winner. I had pictured myself at the concert, too. Somehow, though, I hadn't gotten it right. Maybe I wasn't as good at manifesting as I thought.

After a period of reflection, I realized that while I was telling myself I wanted to win tickets to the Ray Lamontagne concert, there was more to it than that. In fact, what I *really* wanted – and was trying to manifest – was twofold: not only did I want to win tickets from the radio station, but I also wanted to attend the concert with "someone I adored who also adored me." (NOTE: I was single at the time.) Oye. Okay, not insurmountable, but definitely a bit trickier for the Universe to respond to.

The point is, if I had avoided the rookie mistake of trying to manifest winning tickets from this one particular radio station, and acknowledged the additional emotional longing in my dream, I could have focused on manifesting attending the Ray Lamontagne concert for free – with someone else – and opened up dozens more avenues for how it all came to be.

Here are some more generic examples:

» Do you want a raise at work, or do you want to be a lot wealthier than you are now? A raise is pretty specific and doesn't give the Universe much room for creativity. Saying you want to be *wealthier than you are now*, however, lets the Universe figure out the best way to bring more wealth into your life be it via a raise or bonus, a monetary gift, a sweepstakes, or even a new dream job with a much higher salary.

» Do you want to lose weight, or do you want to *love how you look and feel*? One presupposes that the number on the bathroom scale is what matters, whereas the other allows room for options such as losing inches instead of pounds, becoming more self-compassionate and suddenly falling in love with your body exactly as it is, or even having plastic surgery to embellish your features in such a way that you feel fabulous forevermore.

» Do you want a larger group of friends, or do you want to feel less lonely? Having a larger group of friends doesn't necessarily mean that someone will always be available or that you'll feel loved, but wanting to feel less lonely allows the Universe to deliver options that may address your need to be with people without having to befriend them. Those things could include a perfect-for-you volunteer opportunity, a weekly meet-up group, or being asked to chair an important and sizeable event for your community.

Hopefully by now you're getting an idea that there are different ways to manifest and the results can vary significantly. Read on, though, because there's more...

Specific or Loose?

It's your choice to be specific or loose when it comes to manifesting. There's a difference between wanting a new car and wanting a new Honda Civic Coupe. Same goes with wanting a fulfilling romantic relationship, versus hoping the sexy intern with whom you work will go out with you. As you can imagine, there are benefits and drawbacks to manifesting from each perspective.

I'll use myself as an example, specifically when I wanted to buy my last new car. At the time, I had an idea that I wanted to trade my Toyota Corolla in for a Honda Civic. I began researching Hondas, and created a spreadsheet that listed their average prices, features, re-sale values and more. I even decided to download a picture so I could see the car each time I added new information to my sheet. At the time, I thought I wanted a black Civic, but alas there weren't any photos of black Civics on the Honda website. So I grabbed a shot of what they did have: silver.

After a couple weeks of visiting various dealerships in town, figuring out who would give me the most money for my traded-in Toyota, and who had the best offers, I settled on one particular dealership. At that time, Honda Civics were in high demand, so most of the dealerships where I

The Pocket Guide to Manifesting

lived didn't have more than one or two on the lot and the ones they did have were already spoken for. If I wanted a black Honda, I'd have to wait for the next truckload to arrive and my name would be on a list. The entire process could take three or four weeks. Well, despite all of that, I figured I'd test drive whatever they had in stock to make sure I loved it as much as my research told me I should.

So I went to my dealership of choice, and they offered to bring around the one Civic they had that wasn't yet spoken for. As the guy drove around the building and pulled up to me, I found myself thinking, "That is one sexy-looking car!" It wasn't black, though; it was silver, just like the one I'd been staring at on my research spreadsheet. Here's why: although I originally thought I wanted a black Civic, my subconscious was manifesting silver because that's what matched the image I'd been staring at on my spreadsheet!

When I got back from my test drive, I knew *that* was my new car. I bought it and have loved it ever since. Way to go, Universe! Thanks for knowing me better than I know myself!

As I've cultivated more of a manifesting mindset through the years, my attitude has definitely shifted from specific to general, kind of a "Hang Loose, Dude" approach. By that I mean that I tend to focus broadly on what I'm wanting and let the Universe fill in the details. Part of this may be because I'm not as fussy as I once was and recognize that I can be happy under many different circumstances. Another part might be because I've come to know the Universe as a great order filler, with a terrific knack for giving me what I don't always know I want until after it appears.

See, I'm not as visually creative as some people are. My brain is good at choosing between Choice A and Choice B, but throw in C, D, E, and F and I start to get confused and/or worn down. And while some people are great at "creating from a blank slate," that's not my forte. I've been in group visualizing exercises before where people have said things like, "I visualized the house I'd like to buy, and could see every last detail down to the spider on the bedroom ceiling…" Meanwhile, I'm thinking, "I'd be lucky to see the ceiling!" With that in mind, I tend to fall back on what I've *already* seen, known, or done and use those as benchmarks. Therefore, I don't always know what would delight me because I have a finite set of experiences from which to draw. The Universe, on the other hand, is infinite and has filled my life with incredible experiences I never could have dreamed of in such exact detail.

Using the house as an example, when I manifested my first (dream)home, I didn't ask for it to be a certain color, in a certain neighborhood, or be a certain style, or even to have a certain number of rooms. I was much looser, instead relying on adjectives that described how I wanted the house to feel to me: safe, spacious, well-built and easily maintainable with lots of natural light, room for guests, and cool neighbors.

The result? I manifested an incredible house that had features I wouldn't have conceived of on my own, such as an exercise room on the first floor with a huge picture window to gaze out of, a half-bathroom off the kitchen, a gigantic storage room, and beautiful carpeting throughout (you can read the *full* story in the Appendix!).

All that is to say that it's up to you whether or not you want to be specific or more general when you're drawing to you the stuff of your dreams. One could argue that the generalists are more successful manifesters because they don't care what they get and would be happy with anything. That's not entirely true, but it's also not wholly incorrect. I've had success manifesting from both standpoints, but like I said, I tend to approach it more generally than when I first started in my late 20's.

STEP THREE:
Feel As If You Already Have Whatever It Is You Want

If I could attach sound to this book – where lots of sirens, bells, or other raucous noises would go off – it would be right here! Why? Because *feeling as if you already have whatever it is you want* is THE MOST IMPORANT STEP IN MANIFESTING! Simply stated, our emotions are like throwing gasoline on a fire when it comes to manifesting. Whatever we've decided we want, how we're feeling when we're thinking about those things determines how quickly – and sometimes even *if* – they're coming our way.

Anytime I've manifested something significant, it's because I've been able to step into an emotional state – *prior* to receiving what I wanted – that matched how I would feel when I received that thing. Remember earlier when I said that I'm not as visually creative as other people? Thankfully, I *am* emotionally creative. I know a good feeling when I've had one, and I can replicate the same sensations in my body with very little prompt. It's probably a riot for those around me to witness me at my manifesting best: prior to receiving what I want, I practice excitement, elation, jubilation and mentally high-five the Powers that Be, shouting "Thank you, Universe! Thank you!" over and over with a big smile on my face. The neatest part of it is after I've received the thing I wanted to manifest, I actually DO feel those same feelings and begin, at that point, audibly shouting, "Thank you, Universe! Thank you, thank you, thank you!"

I once walked out of a meeting with a close friend of mine who told me that prior to arriving at the meeting two hours earlier, he had manifested how he wanted to feel when it finished. Up until that point, I still relied solely on visualization as the means of getting what I wanted. The meeting we'd been through had been grueling, with those of us in attendance seemingly at odds with one another for the duration. Ironically, we were meeting about a manifesting workshop we were going to co-present. Me? I had visualized the exact details of how I wanted the meeting to go. I knew what I wanted those in attendance to say, think and do. My friend, on the other hand, explained that rather than try to manipulate the details of *how* things might go, he preferred to let the Universe take care of that, and focus, instead, on what he wanted to feel like after-the-fact. He knew if he was feeling good walking out of that meeting, then things would have arranged themselves during the meeting to accommodate his desire.

Sure enough, as we plodded down the stairs post-meeting, he said that he felt satisfied and as if everything worked itself out perfectly. He went on to say that at one point he couldn't have imagined that we'd reach the conclusion we did based on how the meeting was actually going at the time (cut to me panicking as none of the details I'd visualized came into play!), but he held onto his vision – or *feeling*, as it were – and sure enough, everything fell into place for him right at the end.

Now with me, having tried to visualize the details of what would, blow-by-blow, transpire throughout the meeting – let's just say I was woefully let down, not to mention thinking, "God...I SUCK at manifesting! I can't do this workshop!" Little did I know that my friend had just taught me one of my biggest lessons in terms of manifesting best practices: feeling will always get me further than thoughts alone ever could.

I've been following the feeling path ever since.

So what types of feelings am I talking about here? Excitement, elation, surprise, deep contentment, relief, passion, bliss…those are just a few. Basically, it's the *strongest positive emotion* you could imagine yourself having after receiving that which you are trying to manifest. If you're fearful you might get fired from your job, you might manifest extreme relief after a long talk with your boss. If you've been trying to manifest a raise, you might manifest feeling surprised or overwhelmed at your company's generosity. No matter what you are manifesting, however, let me stress again the importance of leaving out the "why" or "how" of arriving at that feeling. The specifics – why you didn't get fired or just how much more money you will earn – are for the Universe to figure out!

Once, I took a spontaneous road trip to surprise a guy I had a crush on. He played in a band that would be performing five hours away, and I thought, "Hey, great opportunity for a road trip!" I had no idea if he'd be receptive to seeing me or how things might go, but rather than get caught up in a play-by-play, I simply jumped to how I wanted to feel from the time he saw me arrive through the end of that road trip. So I settled on feeling extreme gratification with his response to my surprise visit, then bliss, and then increasing joy as each moment of the trip unfolded.

Sure enough, from the moment I arrived at my destination and our eyes met that's exactly how it all played

The Pocket Guide to Manifesting

out. He was thrilled to see me and totally, joyfully surprised, which certainly made me feel grateful about my choice to road trip in the first place. As I listened to his band play over the next few hours, it was total bliss – you couldn't have erased the smile from my face all night if you tried! As the night wore on, all kinds of things happened that I couldn't have imagined. First, I was offered a free upgrade at the bed & breakfast in which I was staying. Then, the morning after the show, the guy I had a crush on invited to tour me around town if I had time. (*If* I had time? You **bet** I had time!) The feelings each of those experiences left me with were exactly what I'd hoped to feel when I was first working my manifesting magic. Our emotions truly are super-charged magnets for materializing what we want!

Now, funny enough, as I was writing this section of the book, the same friend who taught me about the importance of feelings in manifesting called me to ask for a quick coaching session before an important meeting. As an events producer, each year he must ask a board of directors for funding for an event series he's in charge of. By all accounts, the board loves him, yet every year they seem to have less and less money to spend on his events. He was dreading this meeting and had spent the previous days envisioning conversations with various board members that always ended in statements such as, "We love the work you do, but unfortunately, we can only give you $X,XXX this year."

I listened to my friend and then reminded him that *he* was the one who initially taught me what I was about to gift back to him. "Forget about what's happened in the past. Forget about the individual players and what they might say. Jump to how you want to *feel* once the meeting is over. As you're walking to your car, maybe you're feeling total satisfaction, thinking to yourself, 'Wow, that was AWESOME! They finally understand how important this event series is and are willing to back it up financially. Yeah!'" I went on to say that by playing things out in his head based on previous experiences, he was simply cementing everyone into their old roles, which included him as the receiver of less and less money each year.

Now, he knew all of this already, but isn't it funny how sometimes we simply need reminding when the stakes feel particularly high for us? Anyhow, he called me when the meeting ended and said that he left the meeting feeling exactly how he'd manifested he'd feel. In fact, the meeting had gone along as it always did right until the end, as some of the board members were getting up from their chairs and leaving the room. That's when someone said, "Hey, we love this guy and what he does, so why don't we meet again to talk about giving him some extra money this year?" My friend was elated! He couldn't have seen that coming, and it left him feeling just how he'd manifested when everything was said and done: good *and* surprised!

Hold On To That Feeling!

After identifying how you want to feel once you've manifested something, it's important to stay in that "feeling space" anywhere from a few seconds to a minute or two. According to the channeling work of Esther Hicks (Abraham-Hicks), the optimal time to spend in a feeling space is 17 seconds.

From my experience, you'll know when you've achieved what I call emotional magnetization – whether that takes 17 seconds or not – because it's like your entire energy shifts. You'll experience a physiological reaction that may send shivers throughout your body, warmth throughout your veins, or a deep, contented sigh from your lips. Sometimes, as I'm working my manifesting magic, I actually feel as if I've created a wave-effect, pulling what I want toward me, effortlessly and quickly. And indeed, I feel energized and intensely alive!

When I manifested the near-million dollar job offer, I actually felt as if I was already a millionaire for a few seconds. Something in me shifted as I went from "Megan who earns $45,000 a year" to "Megan the millionaire!" I had sensations I'd experience if money was no object and I could easily afford anything and everything I desired. Those feelings didn't last long, granted, but in that case, they didn't have to. I simply needed to change my then vibration from "life as it's always been at xyz amount of money" to "life as it would feel at XYZ amount of money!!!"

Here's another example – one of my favorites, actually – that exemplifies the importance of feeling in order to draw to us what we want. It involves the romantic weekend tryst I spoke of earlier. It was late August at the time, and I was talking with a friend about the state of my romantic life. I was lamenting that I really didn't *have* a romantic life, and how nice it would feel to have someone or something to look forward to.

Shortly after our conversation, I decided that complaining wouldn't change my situation (contrarily, it might cement it). So I decided to work some manifesting magic, beginning with affirmations (read all about the power of affirmations in Section 3). I began repeating to myself, "My life is full of the greatest passion and romance imaginable! I have the *best* love life, with the *greatest* guy and am having so much fun!" I used that phrase for a few days to rewire whatever was going on in my brain that had me stuck believing I lived an unromantic life. Then, a week before Labor Day Weekend, I decided that affirmations needed to be backed up by some faith-based behaviors. So I opened up my electronic calendar and blocked off the quickly approaching holiday weekend and wrote, "Most Incredible, Passion-Filled, FUN, Romantic, Sexy Weekend Ever with the Most Awesome Guy!!!"

Now, let me put this in perspective. At the time, I didn't have any love prospects on the horizon, so if blocking off an entire weekend on my calendar was pretty ballsy, then blocking off a three-day holiday weekend was just plain nuts. The one guy who might have fit the bill was a former boyfriend who was out of the country at the time and wouldn't be home for months. Complicating that was the fact that I'm also rather shy and have a tough time asking guys out, not to mention the fact that I also wasn't big into the social scene, preferring to stay home most weekends. Anyone looking at my situation from the outside would have thought I was crazy, but I knew better.

Beyond just blocking off Labor Day Weekend on my calendar, I started getting excited about a possible tryst, and here's where the proverbial rubber met the road. I felt positive anticipation and "whoo-hoooooooooooo" energy pulsing through my veins as I envisioned how awesome such a weekend could be. As my excitement grew, my body chemistry changed. Endorphins were released and my heartbeat quickened. I was smiling without realizing it and could see myself mouthing, "Thank you, Universe. Thank you!" over and over again. With every fiber of my being, I felt as if my manifestation had already come true.

The next thing I did was to take action – small action, mind you, but action nonetheless. Thankfully I've learned that the size of our actions doesn't dictate the size of our return. (Remember, I like things easy!) One action may seem completely unrelated to our ultimate goal, but that's the beauty of manifesting: since we don't know from where or how our dreams will come into being, we can literally do *anything* so long as it puts us out into the world where the Universe can find us and take care of the rest. It's even better if we choose to do something we truly love while manifesting, because when we're *already* doing something we love, our vibration is sky high, and we become magnets for even more stuff we love.

My choice was to attend a concert that upcoming Friday night with a buddy of mine. I love live music; it thrills me. So when a friend suggested we go out together for a drink, I chose a location that featured live music. I even visualized, before we got to the show, interacting with a member of the band. I didn't know this band from Adam, so it was a funny visualization, to say the least. Anyhow, when we arrived and I first laid eyes on the band, I was instantly smitten with the mandolin player. He was gorgeous in a way that gets things stirring deep within me, with an energy I admired. After the second or third song, I leaned over to my friend and whispered, "Given the chance, I would do naughty, naughty things with that guy..." My friend, surprised to hear me talk like that, shockingly replied, "REALLY?" with a big smile on his face.

After the show, completely uncharacteristic of me but at my buddy's insistence, I said hello to the mandolin player and struck up a quick conversation. Too shy to do much more, I went home that night kicking myself for not taking bolder action. Fortunately, thanks to Facebook, I was able to send him a message telling him just how dreamy I thought he was. I figured whether or not it led anywhere

The Pocket Guide to Manifesting

didn't matter; I had taken action – *any* action – in honor of putting some romance back into my life.

Now, that same night I also received a surprise email from a different guy – let's call him "West Coast Guy" – from whom I hadn't heard in quite some time. He was someone I met four years prior and on whom I'd had a H U G E crush. Unfortunately, we lived on opposite coasts and the timing was never right, so we'd all but lost touch. However, his email, which talked about how he wanted to add more pleasure into his life, gave me just the window of opportunity I needed. So once again, rather uncharacteristically, I took action. I wrote him a reply and in it, I invited him to spend a pleasure-filled weekend with me. Now, the weekend I was referring to wasn't Labor Day Weekend, the one I'd put a line through on my calendar, indicating terrific romance with an awesome guy; it was the one before, the one beginning the *next day*. The following morning, he wrote back and said that while he was flattered and intrigued, he couldn't make it work. I let him know that was fine, and if he changed his mind, he should reach back out.

At that point, I revisited my "Most Romantic Weekend EVER!" manifestation, since Labor Day Weekend was, by then, just seven days away. Undaunted by my seeming misses, I focused on feeling the excitement of having something spectacular to look forward to, and saw myself mouthing, "YES, YES, YES! Thank you, Universe! Thank you!" to the sky. I was smiling and giddy despite the seeming letdowns that surrounded me. I could feel my manifestation coming true! (Side note: the mandolin player, flattered by the email I sent him the night of the show, had invited me to swim with the band the morning after, before they headed back home; me, being nervous about his hotness and feeling unsure about my swimming prowess and bathing suit readiness, politely declined... and yes, in hindsight, all I could think was, "Damnit, Megan!")

A short while later, West Coast Guy emailed again. He'd had a change of heart and wondered if my offer was still good, only could we do it Labor Day Weekend, instead? I instinctively stopped reading his email, felt a big smile stretch across my face, looked up at my ceiling and began excitedly saying, "OH MY GOD, THANK YOU, UNIVERSE! THANK YOU, THANK YOU, THANK YOU!"

That weekend, true to what I'd envisioned and felt, was one of the most incredible, passion-filled, FUN, romantic, sexy weekends I'd yet had, and it was spent with the most awesome guy imaginable, whom I couldn't have known would be the right guy to ask for in my manifestation. The Universe knew, though, and when all was said and done, he was the only guy I could have pictured experiencing that level of bliss with at the time.

So, as often as you can, remember to leave things to the Universe because it is *far* wiser than you or I will ever be.

Basically our only jobs are to manifest through emotions, and then take a couple small, fun actions that let the Universe work its magic.

STEP FOUR:
Let the Universe Figure Out Delivery Options

One of the biggest stumbling blocks people new to manifesting have is what Mike Dooley refers to as the "dreaded how's." Too often people can't separate the manifesting of their dreams from the *idea of how* their dreams could come true – meaning in what form or via what avenue they might be delivered. When this happens, people tend to block the true magic of manifesting.

Remember earlier when I was describing what manifesting is, and I used the pizza analogy? Manifesting is deciding you want pizza, but not making or ordering one for yourself, and yet somehow your doorbell rings and it's a pizza delivery guy holding a fresh, hot pizza for you. Well, this is just one of the many ways that a pizza might be manifested. Maybe, instead of a deliveryman at your door, it's your neighbor stopping over because two pizzas instead of one were delivered to his house and he wondered if you wanted some. Or maybe you decide to go for a walk and they are giving away free pizza at the Little League game in the town center.

The point here is that when you're manifesting the life of your dreams, or any tiny segment thereof, it is absolutely

NONE OF YOUR BUSINESS how the Universe makes any of it happen. Your only jobs are to know what it is you want, and to remain an active participant in life, meaning you can't just go to sleep from now until your dreams come true. You have to keep living day to day and going about your daily routines.

What happens when people can't separate from the "how's?" Well, take for example the time when a friend of mine wanted to attend a party and bring a date and I told her to manifest the perfect guy (she had about a week to do so). She responded cynically because in her mind there were only two guys who would ask her out, and one was her ex-boyfriend. So she resigned herself to the idea that while she wanted a date to the party, she would probably go alone.

In this particular example, my friend negated the magic of manifesting by assuming that there were only *two* possible avenues the Universe could travel in fulfilling her wish: either her ex-boyfriend or the other guy she knew. She failed to acknowledge the myriad other ways a date could manifest, such as meeting someone new at a store or in the coffee shop she frequented. She didn't consider that perhaps a friend would suddenly want to set her up on a blind date with a terrific guy, or that someone she hadn't seen in years might suddenly reappear in her life. So what happened? You may have guessed that she did, indeed, end up going to that party alone, but from a manifesting standpoint, I'm not convinced she needed to.

Another example: a different friend of mine wanted to

increase his income. At the time, he was writing and self-publishing specialty books. In his mind, the only way he could increase his income was if he printed and sold more books, so that's what he visualized: selling more books. Ultimately he did manifest selling more books; it wasn't, however, enough to bring in the level of income for which he hoped. My advice to him was to let go of *how* his income might increase – to move beyond the idea of *just* selling more books. Rather, I encouraged him to imagine that his bank balance was suddenly much higher than it had ever been. Forget *how* and instead leave it up to the Universe to figure out. After all, *any* money that comes in is IN-COME. While he may have thought it could only come from his current job, other possibilities included:

» Being gifted a sum of money (think bonuses, bequeathments, etc.)

» Finding out a utility bill was overpaid and receiving a rebate

» Being offered a short-term, high-paying freelance job out of the blue

» Being asked to participate in a paid focus group

» Winning the lottery (everyone's favorite standby)

» Having someone admire something he owned and then offering to pay him twice what it was worth

» *Insert a hundred other examples here because the Universe is that clever!*

It is remarkably important to release how we think something might happen when we're in the midst of manifesting, especially if we want to let the Universe do its best work. Remember one of the earlier guidelines I mentioned about keeping an open mind? That's what this step entails. As humans, our brains can only construe a finite set of possibilities when it comes to figuring out how our dreams may manifest. The Universe, on the other hand, is unlimited and, for what it's worth, exceptionally sharper than we are! Why not simply worry about our job – figuring out what we want – and let the Universe figure out how to deliver it?

PART THREE:
The Roles of Visualization & Affirmation

Picture (It) Perfect(ly) – Visualization

Some people say visualization is a really important aspect of manifesting. I don't disagree, but I don't rank it as highly as I do being able to step into the feeling space associated with what I desire. Then again, I'm not a hugely visual person as I mentioned earlier. I'm more of a feeler.

One of the main reasons I don't rank visualization higher than feelings is because often times, I think, the more visual we get with something, the more *specific* we're asking the Universe to be with the *what* and *how* of the deliverables. And remember, getting caught up in "how's" is a big no-no in manifesting.

For instance, if I'm visualizing being asked on a date, and I see an email invitation arriving in my inbox, I've already limited how that date invitation might arrive. Not to say it won't, can't, or *shouldn't* arrive via email, but as I said earlier – and this bears much repeating – I do NOT want to try telling the Universe how to do its job! I only know a handful of ways things might be done, a far cry from the billions possessed by the infinitely intelligent Universe. I'd rather go right to feeling, frankly, and let surprise, excitement, and anticipation pulse through my veins while the Universe determines the exact circumstances for bringing those feelings to life.

That being said, there *is* a time and a place in my practice for visualization, and I tend to use it specifically to re-ignite my emotions around a particular subject once they have begun to fade. At times when I'm sensing the need for a prolonged feeling process, visualization both enhances my focus and increases my stamina for holding a feeling. This, in turn, makes the feeling more *real* in my experience, thus promoting a swifter manifestation.

Let's get to an example. One morning – in the shower again of all places! – I used visualization to manifest a raise. It happened like this: I was lathering up my hair as I began envisioning a scenario with my boss, whom I'd be seeing later that day. I pictured myself walking into his office, and after the usual pleasantries, hearing him say, "You've been doing such a great job over the past few months. You have taken on more than anyone expected, and as a reward for all of your hard work, I'd like to give you a $5,000 raise." In the visualization, I saw myself with a huge smile on my face. "Oh my gosh, thank you! That's awesome," I said fervently. "Well, you deserve it," he said, smiling back. Then we shook hands and continued our meeting. Now, to set this up a bit better, I hadn't been offered a raise in the two-and-a-half years since I started working for this man. The year before, he did give me a nice cash bonus, but no raise. On top of that, we never even discussed money, and he hadn't brought up any sort of review or salary discussion with me prior to my visualization exercise in the shower.

Now, what do you think happened in "real life?" Well, when I arrived at my boss's office about three hours after my shower manifestation, he was tied up with some other folks so I got to work keeping myself busy. When he came in, he greeted me with the usual pleasantries and then said, "I thought we'd start things off on a high note. I have some good news. The company would like to offer you a $5,000 raise. I know we gave you a cash bonus last year, but this year we chose a salary increase. Everyone feels you've been doing a great job and you've more than earned it."

My reaction was immediate and fervent just like I'd manifested it. I smiled and excitedly responded, "Oh my gosh, thank you so much! That's awesome! Wow!" We then shook hands and continued our meeting.

You can clearly see the role that visualizing played in the experience with my boss: focusing my energy, centering my emotions, and creating a clear picture of this particular scene. And again, within a few hours this manifesting exercise produced tangible results.

Someone once asked me, after I shared this story, whether I thought I truly did *manifest* that raise, or if I might be psychic and actually *saw* what would happen before it transpired. I didn't respond definitively one way or the other – I *have* had some pretty intuitive experiences in my life, as well – but I did say that it's not the first time things have happened this way!

I've also used visualization as a means of manifesting in my romantic life. Once, when I wanted to manifest the kind of romance that others admire, I imagined myself walking arm-in-arm with my guy, looking so adorable together that people we passed on the street felt compelled to comment. Sure enough, a few weeks later, I happened to be with a terrific guy, enjoying a romantic day, strolling arm-in-arm down the street and past a park. A lady called out to us and said, "You two are adorable together!" Just like I had visualized.

Still another time, after being pulled over for speeding, I visualized that rather than being issued a ticket, I was let go with just a warning. After handing my license and registration to the police officer, I sat back and got to work imagining my ideal scenario. I saw him running my information through the system, finding no prior infractions, and then returning to me and saying, "Please, just slow down." I anticipated my relief and saw myself nodding and thanking him. Sure enough, he walked back over to me and gave me a warning. Happily I nodded, said, "Yes, sir," and thanked him before continuing on my merry way.

There are many ways to help you visualize your desired outcome. Throughout the years, I've tried several, sometimes switching between them depending on what felt right in the moment. It's not an exact science, so my advice is to play around and have some fun before picking the one that feels best to you in your current manifesting situation.

In-Action Visualizing

"In-action" visualizing is when, no matter where I am, I flash forward to the future and get all excited about whatever it is I'm about to do or experience at that point (rather than the point I'm actually in). For example, one day I was driving in my car and decided to use my 45-minute commute to manifest a few things, one of which was a hot date with a great guy I'd be really excited about meeting.

I'd recently been having very lukewarm reactions to the guys with whom I was coming into contact and decided enough was enough. Although I didn't have any prospects on the horizon at the time, I nonetheless pictured that I was driving to that hot date, and was super excited about the guy I'd be meeting. For the next thirty seconds, I was no longer commuting but was *driving to that date*. I could feel the excitement pulsing through my veins, along with a butterfly-inducing nervousness that comes from really great about-to-be experiences, the types of emotions a person feels when they know they're headed for BLISS. I was also mentally thanking the Universe over and over. Once I was done manifesting, I refocused on my actual commute.

About two weeks later, I found myself in the car, having the *exact* experience I'd previously visualized and felt. The time in between, I hadn't done anything extraordinary to bring the guy or the date about. I simply trusted in my visualization, threw out a feeler or two (aka, cast a couple lines into the proverbial Universal waters), and then let the Universe do the rest. True to form, that led me to actually driving to meet an incredible guy for a super hot date. Bliss barely began to touch upon what I was feeling!

Vision Boards

Vision boards are another useful way of visually bringing things to life. They can be anything from hand-drawn sketches to intricate collages of brightly colored pictures from the Internet, magazines, books, or private photo collections. As depicted in the beginning of this book, I've also created word-only vision boards that feature my manifestation subject (i.e., New Friends) and a series of adjectives describing that subject's particulars (i.e., fun, loving, supportive, open-minded). In some cases, I include a picture of myself alongside the things I want to manifest – to make sure I'm part of it – while in others I just trust the visuals themselves to inspire me.

Most importantly, I refer to my vision boards regularly

or post them in places where I will frequently see them. For a while, I kept my vision boards as separate collages taped to my kitchen cupboards. Since I was often in my kitchen, they were permeating my subconscious on a daily basis, reminding me of the things I would be bringing into my life. And having them separate – as in categorized by "Romance," "Dream Home," "Friends" or "Career" – helped to keep me clear and let me focus in on just one if I felt like doing so.

I also learned to keep my vision boards fresh, since my desires flex and evolve with time. In the case of my (dream)home, when I was in my 20's I desperately wanted to live by the ocean; in my 30's, though, this wasn't as important to me, so I updated the images surrounding my dream home in my collage. Finally, when I switched to a word-only collage, that's when the magic happened.

Mirror Writing

The bathroom mirror is an excellent place to practice visualization. For starters, it's where we see a reflection of ourselves at least a few times throughout the day. By writing what we'd like to visualize around our reflection, it's almost as if the things we want then surround us in "real time," making them more palpable and perhaps even inevitable.

When using this technique, dry erase markers work well to mark the mirror up in such a way so that whenever I'm gazing at myself, I'm also "covered in visions" of what

I most want. I can also size up if the words or images I've chosen feel right or resonate on any given day, and if not, I can easily change them so they do.

Creative Renaming

A friend of mine taught me this one. Not only did it make me laugh, it also made good sense! Whenever she was on the tail end of a relationship with someone and wanting to manifest the next best one, she'd edit the name of the person she was currently with in her cell phone to "Someone Better Is Coming Along." That way, whenever that person would call, she had an immediate visual reminding her that the person she wanted to manifest was *on his way*!

In a similar vein, another friend called her ATM card her "Magic Card." Rather than seeing the piece of plastic she used to pay for things tied to an exhaustible supply of money in her bank account, she envisioned that the card was magical enough to connect her to infinite funds for whatever she desired, and that money would *magically* appear on the card, making her feel consistently wealthy. Sure enough, that's how it worked out! Large sums of money came her way effortlessly; her "Magic Card" always had more than enough to cover what she most wanted and needed.

Media-Inspired Visions

Watching movies and television shows or reading books that

The Pocket Guide to Manifesting

depict the scenarios I'm after has also helped me focus my attention on the stuff of my dreams. This approach is pretty straightforward. Wanting a lighthearted romance? Watch a romantic comedy. Desiring significant wealth? Read a book whose protagonist is wealthy. Craving an exotic vacation? Do a Google search and find pictures of cool places around the world.

At one point in my life, just before entering a significant long-term relationship and after having been single for awhile, I was watching the television show *Frasier*. One of the main characters, a psychologist named Niles, had been pining for his brother Fraiser's live-in housekeeper, Daphne Moon, for six years. Although he loved her deeply – *worshipped* her, in fact – he was always too afraid to actually act out his desire.

As I watched the show, I remember thinking how nice it would have been to have someone pine for and worship me that same way. There was one scene, in particular, after Niles and Daphne got together, during which Daphne told a friend how amazing her life felt now that she and Niles were together. The way she described being loved by, and being in love with Niles, resonated so strongly with me that I had tears in my eyes and I remember thinking, "Yes, yes, yes! That's how I want to feel, too!" Just a few weeks after watching that episode, I ended up falling in-love with a former coworker. We'd known each other for six years and he later confessed that he'd been enamored with me for the entire time. In fact, he'd wanted to ask me out quite a few times since we'd met, but always felt it'd be the best thing for him and the worst thing for me. Thankfully he overcame his fear, and we were able to spend a couple wonderful years together.

Say What? – Affirmations

Affirmations are phrases that can be written, thought about, spoken aloud, or all of the above. They reinforce what we currently believe about something that exists in our lives, and they are great for retraining us to think positively instead of negatively. For instance, in my early 20's, prior to becoming a happier, more optimistic person, an unconscious affirmation of mine may have been, "I never win anything." On the contrary, a friend of mine had a sister-in-law who won everything. She'd be out playing bingo and return with $500. Anytime she hit a casino, she walked away a winner. Compared to her, I definitely wasn't someone who won stuff. And it was true! It didn't matter if it was a spelling bee or the lottery: I usually didn't come out on top. But was that because I was *actually* unlucky? Or was it because I'd allowed *my thoughts about past experiences of not winning* to actually feed my "I never win" vibration? And more importantly, would my luck have changed if I'd adopted a different affirmation?

Now, no one said affirmations have to be based solely on what is currently seen in our lives. The whole point of manifesting is to shift around our present-day reality and attract a *new* reality that feels even better to us. Affirmations can be future-based or aspirational. In fact, that's how I tend to use affirmations when manifesting. I affirm that I *already* have whatever it is I'm trying to manifest. In the case of my being "unlucky" in my early 20's, if I *really* wanted to win things and become luckier, I might have chosen to affirm, "I am the luckiest girl I know! I win things all the time and it's awesome!"

In my early 30's, when I was still working in the corporate world, I created an affirmation to change the state of my work life. Rather than working 40-50 hours a week at a job where I liked the people much better than the passionless tasks I was completing, I decided I wanted to feel like I was on vacation each day. You know that feeling, right? It's the one where you wake up in the morning and your time is your own. Maybe you're in an exotic location, or just somewhere you really love. You feel happy, light, and excited to start the day because you don't have any responsibilities except the ones you create for yourself. On top of that, you feel good money-wise – because hey, you're on *vacation*, not *unemployed*. That's how I wanted to feel every day, so I crafted the following affirmation:

Every day feels like I'm on vacation! I'm doing what I want, when I want, with the people I want, in ways that I want, in the places I want, am getting paid what I want and I'm having so much fun!

I repeated this affirmation everyday for probably a year. I kept it on a little sticky note taped to my desk so I'd be reminded of it whenever my eyes caught a glimpse. Then I switched it to an electronic reminder, which popped up on my computer each day, reminding me of what I wanted to manifest. Then one day after I'd been promoted at my corporate job and was sitting in a hotel room overlooking the skyline of San Francisco, California, it dawned on me: I really *did* feel like I was on vacation everyday.

See, as part of that promotion I negotiated a terrific pay raise that was higher than the company initially wanted to offer me ("getting paid what I want"). I was traveling all over the country to cities I'd always wanted to see, visiting various offices ("in the places I want"). I was working alongside new and positive people who were a lot of fun ("with the people I want" and "having so much fun"), and I made my own schedule for the most part ("when I want"). It had all fallen into place and I'd barely noticed! It wasn't until I was sitting in that hotel room in the City by the Bay, writing an email to my brother, that it all clicked.

The "How To's" of Affirmations

When it comes to affirmations, here are a few helpful hints to keep in mind. We'll call these the "Three Stays":

- » **STAY POSITIVE.** First of all and most importantly, use positive language. In other words, make sure to state what you DO want, as opposed to what you DON'T want. Words *absolutely* affect how our minds process likely outcomes and what we're drawing into our experiences. I once read that in the process of manifesting, the Universe doesn't understand negating words in a sentence, but instead focuses on everything else. Here's what that means: In the sentence, "I don't want to be poor anymore," the Universe skips over "don't" and responds only to "be poor." End result? Probably the *opposite* of what was desired! One better way to word that statement would be, "I want to be rich."

Another example, "I wish I wasn't sick," just affirms and manifests more sickness because the Universe doesn't understand the word "wasn't." Try "I want to be healthy" instead.

Another way to put this is to make sure you're thinking, speaking, and wording things in the *positive*, as opposed to trying to *get rid of* a negative. This is the fine line on which manifesting dances. For instance, let's say I'm trying to manifest feeling happy because I've been a little depressed lately. I have some choices: I can focus on getting rid of the depression, or I can focus on feeling happier. Seems like flip sides of the same coin, but the very things we focus on, or better yet our awareness of "what is," are the things we get more of. So if I focus on taking away depression in order to feel happier, what I'm really doing is *strengthening depression*. If, however, I shift my focus onto wanting to be happier – ignoring that I may feel depressed right now – my focus goes there, and I add energy to happiness, allowing it to manifest in my life.

- » **STAY PRESENT.** Second, keep affirmations in the present tense! Doing this tricks our brain into thinking that we already have whatever it is we're affirming, as opposed to making it think we have to wait for a future date to get it. For instance, saying "I am in the best relationship right now" creates a present-moment connection and, as discussed earlier, shifts our focus and makes us think it's what is. Contrarily, saying "I will soon be in the best relationship…" pushes it out to some nebulous future date that may not ever be achieved. Using the phrase "will be" creates a chasing scenario, where we're always chasing that which we want, but can never catch up to it.

- » **STAY WITH IT.** Finally, remember with affirmations to *keep them top-of-mind* and *revisit them frequently*, either mentally or aloud. Just like with any type of training, repetitiveness helps forge new pathways in the brain that then create new beliefs and habits. I like to write affirmations about my ideal life – either on the computer or on little pieces of paper – and then post them in highly visible places that I'll see everyday. I've created e-calendar reminders, stuck Post-It notes to my refrigerator door, kept index cards in the car, written scrap notes for my wallet, and more. Whatever works, just do it.

PART FOUR:
Additional Tools & Helpful Hints

The four main steps – plus some visualization and affirmation – are the bedrock of the manifesting process. But just like a dancer or concert pianist will develop her own interpretation of a classical style to make it hers, the manifester, too, can add his or her own personal signature to the process. In my years of practice, there are many things I've learned to help move the process along. Here are a few!

Take Action (Any Action!)

One of the greatest things about manifesting is that it actually requires very little effort on my part. In fact, I've found that my biggest effort is remembering that when I want something I can just manifest it! That being said, as the actor Jim Carrey once shared with Oprah Winfrey, "You can't just visualize and [then] go eat a sandwich." You have to take action. *Any* action.

The importance of the word "any" cannot be underestimated. I've come to understand that even when you are manifesting, you simply have to keep living your life and not give up. There should be no sitting and staring at walls during this phase of manifesting! You don't need to know *what* to do, or even *where* to do it. You don't need to know when, how often, or with whom. If you've truly aligned yourself with the manifesting process, these things will intuitively become part of you, leading to the right action at the right time. So trust yourself, trust the Universe, and keep on living!

Mike Dooley uses a great analogy to describe this part of the process. He talks about casting fishing lines into the proverbial Universal waters. Remember my earlier example about manifesting a hot date while commuting in my car? Recall that I didn't do much to bring that experience to life; in fact, I remember hopping onto a dating site probably two or three days after I had my "in action" manifesting experience in the car, and finding two cute guys who matched my search criteria. They were both exceptionally handsome – so much so that I didn't think either was really "in my league" – but I sent each guy a message telling him that he was so attractive that I'd stopped in my tracks. Of course I didn't expect either to reply, told them as much, and simply wished them luck on their journeys. A couple hours later, both had replied and expressed interest in getting to know me better. I hit it off with one of them in particular, and he became my partner for that hot date to which I was driving just two weeks later. And believe me – every feeling I felt while manifesting that day was true-to-life happening as I drove to the date. I had cast two lines, and one came back with a real prize-winner. Pretty simple!

Casting lines was vital in manifesting my dream job as

well. Remember, I only knew how I wanted to *feel* when I was doing my dream job. Despite having some general job titles in mind, I couldn't quite name the position I hoped to land. So I applied to a variety of advertised opportunities that may have fit the bill ever so loosely. In three months, I sent out nearly thirty resumes and even went on some job interviews. I was actually offered one job at a time when I "needed" the money, but because it didn't fit with what I was trying to manifest, I turned it down and kept looking. I *did* end up reaching a point where I threw my hands in the air and thought, "Screw it! This might never happen!" Yes, there are times when even *I* have moments of doubt!

Interestingly, it was at one of these low points when I took a high-paying-yet-disposable seasonal job working outside: shoveling snow. I loved it! It was energizing, invigorating, satisfying, and healthy. But taking that job was also brilliant for other reasons. First, it started flowing money to me once more, which was why I wanted my dream job in the first place. Second, that flow of money once-again established the mindset I was *earning good income* (vital in manifesting things we really want). Third, it was a fun, easy job with people I liked (also integral to the manifesting process). And finally, I wasn't locked into it; I could move on when something that felt even better came along. Sure enough, a few weeks later I was invited to interview for my future dream job. I'd forgotten I'd even sent out that particular resume, but the Universe hadn't. Casting so many lines into the water – which honestly, required very little effort on my part – allowed the Universe to deliver an opportunity that was far better than I could have imagined.

Set Clear Intentions

In the previous examples, you saw how important "casting many lines" was in bringing about a perfect opportunity (and "many" doesn't have to mean hundreds; I found a perfect date with two and a dream job with thirty). But simply casting those lines isn't enough to call the stuff of our dreams with so little effort. The other essential element in this equation is *intention*.

Intention – a determination to act in a certain way – swoops in and makes up for any perceived shortcomings inherent within the efforts we've made on behalf of our dreams. When I say "perceived shortcomings," I actually mean the "how's" that I've encouraged you to overlook all along. Things like misspellings in resumes, grammatically incorrect emails, taking "wrong" turns while traveling to a new place, wearing Outfit A instead of Outfit B to that all-important meeting, etc. As humans, it's as if we've been trained by society to think that all of those details – all of those sneakily disguised "how's" – *actually matter* when it comes to affecting a positive outcome. Yet the world is rife with examples that contradict this supposed truth: the seeming slacker who lands the high-paying dream job, the YouTube video of Nancy Nobody that transforms her into Sally Somebody, the smoker or drinker who outlives the clean-living gym rat.

So what gives? Intention! Yes, *intention* is that super cool energy that flows outward from us and *into the very things we're manifesting.* Used skillfully, intention actually becomes part of what we draw back to us. When we utilize positive intention, it almost doesn't matter *what* we do or *how well* we think we're doing it. Intention is the "fix all" salve that makes up for any misspellings, mistakes, or oversights in our approach. It's the "like attracts like" principle that draws the things we most desire directly to us again and again.

I once sent an email to someone who, in my opinion, was a worthy wordsmith. Although I wasn't quite sure my message to him sounded exactly right (thus setting me up for perceived critique), I set an intention that my message be received with love before I hit "send." I just looked at the screen and beamed love out from my heart and into what I'd typed. A few hours later, I received a response that floored me. Now, I should note that this person had never before used these three words with me in this particular order. He wrote, "I LOVE YOU" back. Although the content of my message to this person in no way beckoned such response, the intention I infused my message with did.

See? It's really very simple. Just inject everything with intention!

Believe Everything is Possible

It bears repeating that part of the splendor of manifesting is knowing that everything is possible. The only limitations the Universe ever knows are the ones we impose upon it with our minds. In other words, our doubts and fears are all that keep what we want – no matter how big or small – from entering our lives.

I was speaking with my neighbor once about some back pain she was experiencing around the base of her spine. Several years earlier she'd had surgery on this area, complete with pins being inserted to keep her spine in alignment. Her current pain had her worried that something had come undone and she'd have to repeat the surgery. This distressed her terribly, so I tried calming her by saying, "Maybe it's not as bad as you think. Maybe some prayers and positive thoughts can help your body heal itself." She responded skeptically. "Well, I *know* this pain because I've had it before. It's just like the pain I felt before the first surgery. I'm just afraid to go get x-rays and then have the doctor tell me that…"

So again I tried to calm her by offering up the miracles of the Universe. "You know I think that whatever we believe we'll see," I said. "So maybe – just maybe – if you shift your thoughts toward believing that you simply strained your back and it will heal itself in a few days, that's what will happen. The body got out of alignment; it can just as easily put itself back into alignment. You just need to urge it along with your mind. And you're prayerful, so light some candles and say your prayers. I will, too." She explained that she *had* been praying, but kept shaking her head like she was convinced whatever was going on with her back was exactly what she didn't want.

I tried one last time. "You know," I said, "there are people who have cured their cancer with positive focused intent, and without the help of western medicine. Miracles happen…" "Yeah," she said, cutting me off. "I believe in stuff like that but think positive thinking and prayers can only get you *so* far…" And so it was. She went to her doctor a couple days later, had x-rays, and was told she'd need a second surgery.

I'll admit that, at times, it's exceedingly difficult to believe *everything* is possible. Our modern culture, especially in the United States, isn't wired to believe in magic, miracles, or even the very best that life has to offer. Instead, we are surrounded by messages to the contrary – negativity, fear, skepticism – delivered via news programs, movies, television, commercials, magazines, and the Internet. No wonder so many of us are pessimistic, doubtful, and resistant to optimism!

According to the channeling work of Esther Hicks, our awareness of what surrounds us tends to dominate our vibration, drawing more of the same towards us. If we're aware of a lot of negativity or limitations, we'll be dogged by these very things; if, however, and we're able to remove ourselves from certain negative situations or stimuli, then things begin to shift. That's why, in my mid-20's, I started training myself away from the so-called mainstream media and teaching myself a new way of thinking, seeing, and believing. I stopped listening to, watching, and reading the news because I realized I could choose whether I wanted its negative influence in my life. In the years that followed, I also distanced myself from other negative stimuli, such as gossipy people at work, cynical friends, unsupportive boyfriends, etc. All of that helped shift my awareness away from negativity. In place of what was negative, I sought positive stimuli in the form of new friends, books, soothing music, nature, open-minded lovers, and more. During that time, my life began to radically change: I had more and more positive experiences and fewer and fewer negative ones.

Keep It Secret

Something I learned through trial and error was to keep the things I was manifesting to myself until they actually materialized. My reasons for this were strictly energetic, meaning that, like it or not, not everyone I shared things with in my early days of manifesting were filled with supportive, positive energy when it came to my dreams. To me, manifesting is like planting a delicate seed that needs to be protected from any harsh elements in order to grow and blossom. Early on, before I realized how precious my dreams were, I'd sometimes share the things I was "working on" with what I now call dream squashers. These were the people who, without missing a beat, would respond with sarcasm or negativity, and proceed to tell me how difficult achieving my desires would be. Now, in a perfect world, such people shouldn't have been powerful enough to dissuade me, but for reasons I won't speculate on here, at times their discouraging words would seep into my subconscious like a poison and destroy the tender seedling I'd just planted. That's when I realized how important it was to only share the things I was manifesting with exceedingly supportive, positive people OR to simply keep it to myself until what I was manifesting had come to pass.

Mind Your Phrases

There are a few phrases I like to use when manifesting to ensure the best possible outcome that's in the highest good for all involved. They are "in a good and balanced way" and "best yet" or "beyond my fondest dreams."

I use the phrase "in a good and balanced way" when I'm manifesting something to ensure that the way in which it's delivered prevents anyone from suffering. For instance, think about the possible ways that increased wealth could be delivered. It could come from a legal settlement that stemmed from an unpleasant situation (an accident, for example), or it could come from joyfully winning a sweepstakes. I'd much prefer the latter. Another example might be increased happiness at work. It might happen because someone with a difficult personality gets fired, thus making me happier, or it could result from my movement to a different, exciting new department. In that instance, no one had to be fired to make my situation better. For me, the phrase "in a good and balanced way" ensures that everyone wins, and that's how I like to keep things.

I use the powerhouse phrases "best yet" and "beyond my fondest dreams" to guarantee that whatever I manifest will be above and beyond the constraints of my mind. This is important because sometimes I *think* I know what a great experience would look or feel like for me, but that's only based on what I've been exposed to, either in my own life or through witnessing it in others. But what if my imagination barely scratches the surface of the Universe's capabilities? It's not worth chancing it, so I use one of those powerhouse phrases to draw to me the ULTIMATE in whatever I'm hoping for.

Notice, also, that I used the word "yet" and not "ever." "Best yet" implies that there's room for the Universe to deliver something even a step or two beyond the current experience at some point in the future, while "best ever" implies that whatever's being sent is as good as it will get. This subtle shift of the wording and subsequent intention can make a colossal difference! Think about it: if I ask for my best job *ever*, and it's delivered to me but doesn't last for the rest of my life, then the *next* job that comes along cannot, by definition, best the previous one. Asking for the best job *yet*, however, gives the Universe future room to play, if need be, and to deliver increasingly better opportunities, as needed or requested.

One last phrase I like to use when I'm considering buying something is "easily affordable by me." I used to say "easily affordable" and leave it at that, until I realized that what one person thinks is affordable might not be what I think is affordable. Therefore, I'd rather play it safe and customize the phrase to fit my own comfort level. When I bought my first (dream)home, for example, I remember the real estate agent telling me that if I could get the house for $XX,XXX, it'd be a steal. Well, what she thought was a steal and what I thought was a steal were two different dollar amounts! The fact that "easily affordable" can be interpreted myriad ways is what led to me adding "…by me" at the end of that phrase.

Be Grateful!

One can never say enough about gratitude. Feeling grateful is a universal panacea – improving our mood, health, outlook, and even our body chemistry. From a manifesting perspective, gratitude is an all-powerful tool that works to reinforce the present as well as expedite the future.

In terms of reinforcing the present, when we take a few moments to recognize and celebrate the things we love in our lives, we're focusing positive energy on those things. And since whatever we focus on grows, every time we give thanks we increase the flow of things we're grateful for into our lives.

For instance, I'm certain that my expressions of gratitude for things I love have kept those things around and strong in my life. I'm grateful for the beautiful roof over my head, for the good coffee I'm drinking, and for the money I have available to me on a daily basis to help me enjoy life and live in a state of abundance. I'm grateful for my good health, for the peace I feel throughout each day, and for the love and appreciation of my friends and family. I'm grateful to be doing what I most enjoy and for feeling fulfilled mentally, spiritually and emotionally. The list goes on!

A terrific quote on present-moment gratitude from Zachary, through Lee Harris, from Harris's book *Energy Speaks*, sums it up beautifully: "...the truth is when you begin to appreciate what you do have, then the Universe will send you more. When you truly appreciate that which you have in your life, be it the people, the work, the roof over your head, then you are surrendered. You are surrendered to the already existent abundance around you." Indeed! Gratitude is one of those indisputable – yet so simple and potent – natural laws that I'm amazed people don't employ it more often!

But gratitude isn't just about the present. It also helps draw the *future* to us faster by helping us act "as if." If there's something you want in your life that hasn't shown up yet, place yourself in the feeling space of thankfulness for that very thing – as if it's already there and you've been enjoying it all along. This involves a bit of imagination. Pretend well enough – with enough feeling (excitement, gratefulness, etc.) – and sure enough, that thing will be yours. In fact, right now I'm expressing gratitude that this finished book was purchased by more people than I dreamed possible in the first few months of release, and that it quickly led to many lucrative offers for future projects. Thank you, Universe! Thank you!

Learn a Little Feng Shui

Whether you believe that energy can be rearranged to create "better flow" or whether you simply believe in the power of intention, the ancient art of feng shui can be a useful tool to usher new energy into your life. The practice involves understanding how to balance energy within a particular space – living quarters, the physical body, or any other contained area – to attract the greatest amount of positivity and establish a freer flowing current around you. (I'm over simplifying this, perhaps, so if it's an area you're interested in a quick search on the Internet will reveal some terrific sources for additional information.) In my eyes, it's the same thing as setting an intention, which the subconscious mind latches onto, thus altering the frequency at which our energy vibrates. There's a saying that goes "energy flows where attention goes," but I'm going to substitute "intention" for "attention." However we set our intention is what determines the type of energy that rushes in to meet us.

Some examples of using feng shui to improve current circumstances include:

» Taping red hearts created from paper, stickers, or whatever material you prefer to the front door of a home to indicate that love resides there.

» Getting rid of anything a former lover gave in order to create space for new gifts and new love to enter your life.

» Always keeping either a representation of a, or a real, $20, $50 or $100 bill in your wallet to indicate constant wealth.

» Wearing a symbol of good health on a chain around your neck to represent the perfect physical condition you're in.

» If you're someone who wants to attract more friends or do more entertaining, making sure you always have extra food and drink on hand for occasions when people stop over.

» Hanging representations of peace, love and joy throughout your home to indicate the positive, happy energy that is always present.

» Putting smiley faces on every check you write to symbolize how happy you are that you always have more than enough money for the things you want and need.

» Dressing the part to *become* the part.

Speaking of that last one, you know how sometimes you can grow so complacent with your life that it starts to show in the clothes you wear, your level of physical fitness, how you do or don't style your hair, what you choose to sleep in each night, etc.? As someone who appreciates comfort and functionality over style, I'd become a predominantly pajama-pant wearing gal who was slowly losing her sense of femininity and sexiness when I crawled into bed each night. It dawned on me one evening as I gazed down at my lounge pants that if I wanted to feel sexier and more womanly – and therefore attract a higher level of that into my life – I might consider buying and wearing some alluring nighties and ditching my frumpier garb. So I did. The first night I wore one of the nighties, I caught a glimpse of myself in the mirror and thought, "MY GOD, why haven't I been doing this all along?!" I felt so attractive and sexy. A few days later, a terrific new love seemed to manifest out of thin air (but ain't that the way, as I've been saying all along?!) and with it, passion and romance became mainstays in my life once again.

Step Beyond Those Material Things

Manifesting isn't just about material gains. I've found that it's also a useful tool for manifesting desired states of mind. Times when I've felt anxious or overwhelmed, I've imagined myself well beyond those emotions and, instead, feeling relieved and peaceful, like, "Ahhhh, yes, everything worked out perfectly and I feel fantastic!" I've manifested improved self-esteem when I'd previously been feeling down on myself. I've manifested improved states of health and in some cases, dissolved physical pain in a matter of minutes. I remember one time I was running on the treadmill, and my ankle was bothering me. I had an on- and off-again ankle injury that started years prior and would sometimes flare up, seemingly out of nowhere, forcing me to quit running for awhile. Determined not to succumb to the idea that I'd somehow manifested pain once more in my ankle, I redirected my thoughts and feelings toward it being completely healed and feeling fantastic. The first ten minutes of the run were tough because the pain was obvious, but I persisted with imagining my ankle completely healthy. Ten minutes after that, all pain had disappeared and I was able to continue on as if I'd never had ankle trouble at all! I just kept imagining myself feeling happy that I could complete my run comfortably, ankle intact, and that's exactly what happened. What's more, my ankle continued feeling perfect from that day forward.

Let Go, Let Go

Letting go, or the ability to set manifesting wheels in motion without worrying whether or not we'll get what we want, is another useful tool in manifesting. This tool acknowledges the fine line that exists between manifesting from a place of desire versus one of lack. When we're manifesting from a

The Pocket Guide to Manifesting

place of pure desire, we don't feel like the thing we want is missing from our lives. We simply think it would be cool to add to all the other great things we have, but, regardless of the outcome, we'll remain happy. The energy at work in this situation is very different from manifesting from a place of lack, in which we believe the thing we want is *absent* from our lives and, until we get it, there is a gaping hole.

So the practice of "letting go" plays a dual role. First, it helps us loosen our grip on the things we want in order to activate the energy of pure desire, versus the energy of "need-it-because-I-lack-it." When we do that, we can more easily jump to feeling like the thing we want is *something we already* have; there's no gaping hole to be filled. It's important to hold our desires lightly in our minds and hearts, trusting that the *things we want also want us*, and will arrive in perfect time and perfect order. This mental shift gives the Universe more breathing room, allowing it the space it needs to fulfill our desires.

There's one more level to letting go. Once we've voiced our desires to the Universe and activated manifesting energies through our thoughts and feelings, we must let go of them completely, affirming our faith that we truly believe in the process. Another way to view this is what I call having the "Fonzie Attitude." For anyone who isn't familiar with the 1970's TV show *Happy Days*, Fonzie was a super smooth, unflappable character who could get what he wanted by snapping his fingers. Women flocked to him, men wanted to be him…and none of it fazed him in the least. He was too cool to care. That's a great way to approach manifesting, and can help accelerate how quickly the stuff of our dreams is drawn to us.

So be like Fonzie and just *let go*! Put out there what you want, and then detach from the outcome and move onto something else, letting faith bring you the object of your desire.

Consider Your Timing

I've had experiences where I've put something I wanted on the calendar and it's come to pass *exactly when I hoped it would*. I've also had the opposite happen, that date coming and going with no result. So what gives? I believe it's finding the right balance between giving the Universe a preferred "due date" and then being flexible about its actual "delivery date."

Forcing the Details

In one of my earlier examples, I talked about manifesting a romantic tryst for Labor Day Weekend that transpired exactly as I'd envisioned. What was it about that example that allowed me to make the timing work in my favor? I wish I could say for sure, but my guess is that the right "players" were already aligned to fulfill my desire and drawing them into my reality was easy once I got into my manifesting groove. The vibration of "fun, exciting, best yet romantic weekend" – without a specific partner in mind, remember –

was like a siren's call that drew to me the perfect person at the time for which I asked.

In other cases, though, it's possible that the element of time is actually a subconscious way of *forcing the details* from a feeling of lack or fear. If I'm trying to manifest money by a specific date, for instance, there's a good chance that I want it by then because I'm fearful of what will happen if it doesn't appear. Same goes with career, good health, etc. When we're *fearful*, we tend to energetically push away the things we want, rather than draw them to us.

Trusting Universal Timing
Maybe it's easier to trust Universal timing because it lets us off the hook. We can put our desires out there, with no particular timetable in mind, and affirm that all will arrive at the perfect time. In my experience, these are far more enjoyable manifesting scenarios because I can, as the saying goes, "Let go and let God" and get on with living my day-to-day life, knowing that what I want will happen in due time.

When I was manifesting my first (dream)home, I danced between trying to control the timing and letting the Universe deliver what I most wanted when it was available. I was in an apartment at the time with a lease that was about to run out. My ideal scenario had me finding my dream home before my lease ran out, and moving into it with just a hint of time to spare. As it turns out, that didn't happen. I was two months away from finding my (dream)home when my lease ended, which meant signing on for another few months and risking having to break that lease. I trusted, though, that however it happened would be alright, and while I had a few sweat-inducing moments in the process – from wanting to control the details, no doubt – ultimately everything worked out perfectly. By reminding myself to wait for everything I wanted to be ready and available to align with my vibratory state – relaxing and releasing my expectations of when it should happen – I learned about trust and liberation at the same time.

Another experience with Universal timing involved waiting in line at airport security the morning of my most important job interview to-date, for that big promotion I talked about earlier. I was flying from the East to West Coast to interview with the president of the company about becoming Director of Corporate Communications. I'd given myself an hour to make it through security and catch my flight, but when I arrived the security line contained four times as many people as I'd ever seen at that airport, even at its busiest!

As I patiently stood in the back of the security line, which didn't seem to be moving nearly as quickly as time was, I heard the people around me panicking. Their flights were taking off around the same time as mine and they were griping about how they weren't going to make it at the rate the line was moving. They kept saying things like, "If we don't get through this line in the next ten minutes, we'll miss our flights." Now, I could have used their predictions and manifested something based on that, but instead I simply visualized myself walking onto my flight with time to spare. I didn't say how much time, nor did I picture myself going through security in a specific number of minutes. I just saw myself getting on my flight, which would depart on-schedule, and arriving on the West Coast in terrific order.

The next thing I knew, a new security officer appeared and opened a special line for some flight-crew members who needed to get through. Then, as if enacting a miracle, the officer waved not to the people in front of me who had been complaining that they'd miss their flight, but to me and about five or six behind me, allowing us to follow the flight crew members into that special, and much shorter security line. I was in and out of it in five minutes, and ended up walking onto my flight with minutes to spare.

PART FIVE: Q & A

Over the years I've been asked many questions by people curious about the manifesting process. Here are of some of the common ones, and my thoughts in response.

Q: *Can We Manifest on Behalf of Others?*

A: My experience tells me that no, we cannot. When we want to manifest on behalf of someone else, we're still really manifesting for ourselves. If we do want to manifest for someone else, however, particularly if they are struggling or stuck in a frustrating situation, it can be done by focusing on the feelings *we'd* like to have once this particular situation has been remedied.

Here's an example: I once knew a friend who was, by choice, living out of his car and had driven from sunny, warm California to bitterly cold New York State in December. At the time he started his journey, he thought he had a warm place to stay upon arrival. Just before reaching New York, though, his accommodations fell through and he didn't have enough money for a hotel. It was far too cold for him to sleep in his car, and since he had two cats with him, I was unable to put him up for a few nights.

Since I couldn't do anything directly to help, I switched into manifesting mode. Rather than manifesting an outcome for him, I manifested myself feeling relieved at news I would receive regarding his situation. I put myself into the feeling space of "Oh my gosh, THANK YOU, UNIVERSE! That's such good news!" I imagined feeling totally at ease, and then just let it go so the Universe could work its magic. A few hours later, he called to tell me that he'd found a place to stay and would be taken care of for the next few days. Thank goodness!

In another example, a friend of mine was taken to court by her ex-husband over shared custody of their children. Her ex-husband wanted sole custody, even though the children were adamantly against the arrangement. It was an important court case for my friend – one that had her thoroughly nerve-wracked and asking for a miracle. On my end, I jumped to the phone call I wanted to receive when all was said and done: hearing her excitedly tell me that she won the case, the judge awarded everything in her favor, and that things went even better than she could have imagined! I heard us laughing together at how amazing the Universe is, and felt incredible relief knowing that she'd made it through to the other side of a difficult situation. Sure enough, the day of the court case, that's what happened. When she called me and shared the good news, at first she was almost in shock at how fantastically it all went. Then we began celebrating as she recounted the details of how the judge awarded things above and beyond what she thought possible. I felt relief and happiness during our conversation, and in my mind, thanked the Universe for its benevolence.

Q: *How Does It Feel When We're Manifesting The "Right Way" vs. The "Wrong Way?"*

A: First, I don't believe that there is a "right" way to manifest. I believe that however we're doing it is the best way at the time. Just be kind to yourself and trust your process. That said, I do acknowledge that there are times when manifesting flows more easily than others, so I'll delve a little deeper.

For me, it's a matter of resistance. I can tell when I'm forcing something or trying to have too much control over an outcome by how it feels when I'm doing it. For example, maybe I'm trying to manifest more money because I recently had an unexpected expense that made me nervous about my available funds for the rest of the month. A big obstacle here is that I'm coming from a place of *fear* (aka, resistance to what is), as opposed to a place of *trust* that all is well and I'm already, always taken care of (aka, having what author Florence Scovel Shinn called "fearless faith"). In this state of outward flowing negativity and fear, I'm restricting the positive energies trying to flow towards me.

In a situation like this, I need to immediately survey my life for examples of my already existent wealth and give thanks for them. I'd look at my beautiful house and give thanks. I'd look at the beautiful furnishings inside it and give thanks. I'd look at my pantry, which is stocked with my favorite foods that I can always easily afford, and give thanks. I'd look at the most recent things I was able to buy without batting an eye and give thanks (i.e., semi-luxury or non-necessity items like body lotions, new sweaters, music, little gifts for friends).

Once I'd done that long enough to bring myself back into a state of feeling wealthy, I'd affirm that I *always* have more than enough money to spend on the things I want *and* need. I'd feel that energy swirling around and in me, and get into the feeling space of having more than enough. From there, I'd ratchet it up a notch and feel as if I had a true windfall of money at my fingertips, causing me to feel really wealthy – like "upper class" wealthy – where I could buy plane tickets to anywhere in the world without thinking twice, afford fine hotels, buy lavish gifts for my friends, etc. I'd then stay in that space of freely flowing positive energy for 15 to 20 seconds and smile at my incredibly good fortune as my feelings altered my previous reality.

Another way I know I'm not in manifesting flow is when I get caught up in – or obsess over – the details. It's like I just can't get them right in my head and I keep adding in more, or changing them, trying to reach a place where whatever I'm thinking about/visualizing/feeling actually feels "right." For example, I remember a few times when I was manifesting a knock-my-socks-off romantic partner, and I knew I wasn't in the right space to do so by how many details I kept throwing in there. My list was as wide as the day is long, including details about his age, physical fitness, body hair, relationship to his mother, which holidays he should get excited about, and more. It's as if I didn't trust myself or the Universe to know me – *to know what I would really respond well to* – and instead had to micromanage the process.

Trying to control so many details is a great, albeit subtle, sign of fear. I've found that when I trust that the Universe knows me better than I know myself, that I can just leapfrog to the highest-existing end result, feel the excitement of its inevitable arrival, and sit back and let it happen. That process is much more natural, and flows more easily than being a detail dominatrix, don't you think? So if you find yourself dealing in details this way, it's a red flag! It's a sign that you fear that what you want won't happen in the best way imaginable. And oh wait, that phrase is exactly what we should jump to from the very beginning! IN THE BEST WAY IMAGINABLE.

Q: *Does Size Matter?*

A: Truthfully, when manifesting, size *shouldn't* matter, but if it does for you, be mindful of the pitfalls of going too big too fast.

One example of this involves a friend of mine who has spent most of his life living at or below the poverty line. For one reason or another, he couldn't work a typical job to help increase his income. Instead, he worked from home for awhile but wasn't successful creating a steady income. Often for him it was feast or famine.

This friend was interested in manifesting and actually got me started on my path. He studied all kinds of techniques taught by gurus around the world and eagerly shared with me whatever he had learned. His big thing was realizing that there was no separation between what he *wanted* and what he currently *had*. In other words, in the blink of an eye or the snap of his fingers he should conceivably be able to create the stuff of his dreams.

One of his dreams was to have a million dollars come his way so, as he put it, he could help feed the hungry. This friend was wonderfully selfless, and envisioned using the million dollars he'd win, inherit, or otherwise draw to him to create a center or foundation through which starving people would be fed. Sounds pretty good, yes? Still, it's been years and he hasn't yet manifested that million dollars, despite his conscious belief that he *should* be able to.

What might be undermining his ability? Granted, this is all speculation, but if I had to guess I'd say it had something to do with his having gone too big too fast, causing deeply rooted subconscious beliefs to be triggered about who or what deserves such a large sum of money, or how that type of wealth gets created.

Each of us holds deep-seated beliefs about money, some of which we may not be aware. Think about how you, personally, view a million dollars. Is it something you can envision yourself with easily? If not, who can you envision having that much money? What types of traits do you think "millionaires" have in common? Chances are, you have a whole back-story put together about millionaires that you're not fully conscious of. Depending on if that story falls into the camp of "anyone can be one" or "you have to be someone special – which I'm not – to be one," it affects your ability to manifest such a great sum of money.

Although my friend was generous with those he loved, in general, he demonstrated pretty impoverished thinking and didn't consider himself a particularly lucky person, one who might, say, win the lottery. He also lived with a partner who appeared fairly cynical (although who or what he surrounded himself with is a topic for another section of this book). Yet he maintained that he wanted to manifest that million dollars.

Looking back, he may have been more successful stepping up to the amount in smaller increments. In other words, had he tried to manifest $100 and been successful (because $100, to some people, feels easier than $1,000,000), that may have given him the confidence he needed to easily manifest $1,000. Once he did that, it would help create new beliefs about how easy it might be to then manifest $10,000, and so on.

The cliché of taking things one step at a time – rather than in a giant leap – is apropos here, but again, only if the thing you're trying to manifest feels BIG to you. For many people, it's important to build confidence in their ability to manifest the stuff of their dreams, so if they're successful on a smaller scale, it often gives them the boost they need to go bigger, and then bigger still.

And oddly, I've also learned that the more we want something, the more we run the risk of reinforcing that we *don't currently have that thing.* What's then triggered is the energy of keeping what we want at bay. So in the case of manifesting something really big, I've found it's more plausible to do so when we're not completely wrapped up in the wanting of that thing.

I understand that might sound strange, but stop for a moment and think about something you really want. For me, at various points in my life, it's been a romantic partner, as you've probably garnered from reading this book. Why was it so important to me? For starters, depending on the timeframe in question, it may have been linked to how long it had been since I had a partner on whom I could count to stick around through thick and thin. In some cases, it had been a LONG-ASS time! Plus, I craved the availability of physical and emotional intimacy with a man about whom I was head-over-heels. When thinking about manifesting a romantic partner in that scenario, then, it would have been from a place of lack: *I wanted it because I didn't have it.* The energy that was getting triggered in that case leaned more strongly toward "I *don't* have" than "I *want* to have," so for me to try and suddenly manifest a romantic partner – or (gasp) a life partner – was at that time, unfortunately, probably just too much.

I know that sounds like it sucks, because isn't the point of this manifesting stuff supposed to be that we can create whatever we want whenever we want it, out of thin air? Yes. And one workaround for having too much desire, as we discussed earlier, is to let go and adopt a "Fonzie attitude." If we can't do that, then suffice it to say we're better off sticking to things we don't have so much "want" for, especially if we want to go big.

Take money, for example. I feel I live a very comfortable, affluent life, so were I to manifest another $5,000 or $10,000 showing up out of the blue, it wouldn't be such a big deal. Part of that is because already I feel like I have a lot of wealth. Notice my use of words there: "I feel." My personal wealth assessment is not compared to or based upon how anyone else might think or feel about money. It's simply the reality of my relationship to what I have and what comes into my life. Plus, I've manifested big chunks of money before, seemingly overnight, so I have the confidence to go as big as I'd like. With romance, however, many times in the past the case had been that I was better off sticking with smaller, more manageable things like weekend trysts until I built up my confidence. Those I knew I could do!

Q: *Why can I manifest some things easily, but others elude me?*

A: As mentioned in the previous section, each of us has areas in life where success comes naturally, as well as those in which we struggle. It could be residue from our childhood or long-held beliefs about our worthiness to receive what we want. Or it could be that, somewhere along the line, an injurious experience shattered our belief in ourselves. The good news is that it's all surmountable. Awareness is a great first step, and allows us to recognize where barriers exist in our minds with regard to manifesting.

For instance, my parents' divorce left me questioning a single woman's ability to live an upscale, enjoyable life. When my father left, I was ten years old. With him left our so-called financial security, as well as my mother's happiness. She struggled to make ends meet, and was frequently physically or emotionally ill or worn out. Seeing her struggle so mightily for many years following her divorce, it's no surprise I unconsciously molded my beliefs around what I saw. As a young woman in my late teens and early 20's, I, too, struggled financially and found myself unhappy a lot of the time. I wasn't in terrific physical health, and frequently felt worn out just like my mom. The idea of having financial security on my own – without a husband – didn't seem possible, so that's how I lived until my mid- to late-20's when I finally started investigating my thoughts. When I realized what I'd been thinking – in other words, when I identified my limiting beliefs – I was able to start turning them around, laying a more positive foundation with affirmations, gratitude, etc. As that happened, I began drawing to me better and better feeling experiences that built up my confidence and helped heal my psyche.

Suddenly I had more money than I dreamed possible, and laughed and smiled so much that people nicknamed me "The Joy Girl." And all of it led me to where I am today, which is to say a happily unmarried woman who owns her own (dream)home and lives life beyond her fondest dreams.

Now, another thing I'll say with regard to being able to manifest some things easily while struggling with others is that every experience we have provides contrast for what we *do* and *don't* want. My friend who won her court case asked me a week after she manifested that miracle what was wrong with her "manifesting men ability?" She knew she had the ability to attract big or important things like beautiful homes and court-case victories, but her dating life wasn't keeping pace. She shared a story about how the most recent guy to ask her out was rather full of himself, not to mention pushy. I reassured her that nothing was wrong with her manifesting abilities, and that all of her less-than-desirable Johnny-come-lately men were simply helping her refine her vision of what she really REALLY wanted. My sense was that the Universe was nudging her to get clearer about her ideal man, and was sending in others to help hone her "manifesting men" skills.

Manifesting, like many other things in life, is a practice and we're constantly given opportunities to fine-tune it. The more we refine, the better we become at drawing to us exactly what we want in all areas of life.

Q: *What if I can't get clear on what it is I really, REALLY want – what then?*

A: It would be nice to think that everyone knows exactly what they want all the time. My experience has shown me, however, that sometimes that's just not the case. When I don't know specifically what to manifest as my ultimate end-result, then I manifest clarity in its place. Sometimes the most I know is how I *don't* want to feel. Maybe I'm worn out, under duress, in a hurry, or have some other experience going on that's making manifesting feel difficult. In those cases, I take a step back and ask for helpful information so I can get clearer, rather than jumping way ahead to a place that, right now, doesn't feel plausible or can't even be imagined.

So for instance, if I'm thinking of starting a new creative project but have no idea what that project might be or how I want to feel about it when it's done, I would manifest an "ah-ha!" moment where the proverbial light bulb goes on above my head and suddenly I know exactly what I need to know to take the next step. That ah-ha moment might have feelings of relief associated with it, or "Ohhhhh YES! That's IT!" excitement.

Any time I don't know what to manifest, I just manifest "knowing." Simple as that.

Q: *I'm going through a tough time right now and feel like I'm stuck in fear and negativity. I worry that, if like attracts like, I'll just keep manifesting more of this. What can I do?*

A: There are times when fear and negativity are inevitable, and we find ourselves in the midst of those energies without realizing how we drew them to us in the first place. If that's the case – and it's certainly happened to me – I recommend doing these two things, as suggested by Joy Holland of *Facets of Joy*:

1. **Use the phrase "Return to Sender, With Love."** This phrase puts an immediate stop to whatever is flowing to us that doesn't feel good. If the negative thoughts and energy we find ourselves in are ours (in other words, belong to us and aren't something we've absorbed empathically from someone or something else), "Return to Sender, With Love" gives that energy a renewed consciousness within us – one that's more positive and love-filled. If the negative thoughts and energy aren't ours – and it's not even necessary for us to know if they are, really – using the phrase reroutes the negativity back to whomever it came from initially and, again, invites renewed, loving consciousness in its place.

2. **Center yourself in love.** The second important step is to center into love. You can either imagine that a pillar of love exists in the center of your being, stretching down into the earth, or you can simply say and intend, "I am centered in love." As mentioned earlier, your intention is what makes it real. The reason we do this is because love is the highest vibration there is, and therefore the most powerful energy on the planet. When we center into love, anything that's *not* love cannot stay in our vibratory pull. It either has to raise its vibration to join us, or has to slink away. Therefore, the experiences around us will shift almost immediately to reflect a higher vibra-

tion, and whatever felt negative or made us fearful will disappear.

Here's an example: At one point in my life, I was involved with someone who alternated unpredictably between the energies of love and fear on a daily basis. When I decided to end my relationship with this person, he reacted badly (aka, fearfully), and severely threatened my well-being. The initial shock I felt caused fear to win out and overwhelm me. Realizing, however, that the state of fear I was in only caused more things rooted in fear to manifest in my life, I began using the phrase "Return to Sender, With Love" as my mantra. I also simultaneously centered into love, remembering that the higher vibration would help shift the reality I was experiencing. In twelve short hours following one particularly fear-filled night, desperation dissolved and tranquility returned to my life. The person who had been threatening me suddenly stopped, and from the new space I found myself in, I was able to manifest my desired end result, which was that he would peacefully leave my life for good. Three days later, that's just what happened. What made it even more miraculous is that just 24 hours prior to me using those two fear-dissolving practices, this same person was threatening to stick around and wreak havoc in my life for another two months!

Return to Sender, With Love, indeed.

PART SIX:
Living Life to Its Fullest.

By now, you've probably gotten an idea that manifesting isn't just something you do when you want one thing to appear in your life. It's what you do when you want *<u>anything</u>* to appear in your life: from experiences to material things. The truth is that manifesting is our natural state of being, a constant process from the time we wake up in the morning until the time we go to sleep at night. When we learn how to direct that process, we notice that life suddenly feels easier and perhaps more fulfilling.

Hopefully you now understand that manifesting is supposed to be fun, too; it's not always about altering some unpleasant reality we no longer want to be in (and you'll recall, even if there is an unpleasant reality, our job is to shift attention to the desired outcome rather than focusing on whatever yucky stuff currently surrounds us…but you're a quick study so you knew that already!). Whether it's a perfect parking spot at a music festival, an amazing vacation, a more positive outlook, greater wealth, or better health, manifesting is our key to putting the amazing powers of the Universe to work for us.

Remember, though, that manifesting is a practice. Be kind to yourself as you get used to creating your world in this way. Stick with it, learn as you go, and celebrate each success. Give thanks to yourself for genuinely remembering how truly powerful you are at your core. Manifesting is *what you do*, and it's *who you are*. Your life is your own design, and now that you know how to attract whatever you want, you can live life to its fullest.

And when that starts happening, you, too, can begin jumping up and down and shouting, "Thank you, Universe! Thank you, thank you, thank you!" on a daily basis for all the greatness that surrounds you.

APPENDIX 1:
More Real Life Examples

Twofer

On a Wednesday evening, I was speaking with a friend in New Jersey about my upcoming trip to visit him for the first time. "You know," I said. "I've been to the Garden State before. I was in college, driving back from a six-week summer program." At one point, I explained, the traffic on the Parkway was backed up for about a mile. Despite the bumper-to-bumper gridlock, I saw a cop in the median, and snarkily thought, "What's he going to do, pull someone over? No one's moving faster than 20 miles per hour!" Sure enough, 30 seconds later, I saw lights flashing behind me. He pulled me over for being in the commuter lane without a passenger in my car. I'd only hopped into it for a second to pass someone else, but that's all it took to get me in trouble with the boys in blue. Needless to say, I thought the violation was ludicrous. So I (eh-hem) sort of ignored it. A couple of months later, however, I got a letter from the State of New Jersey saying, essentially, that I was banned from driving there ever again. For years I retold that story with comedic flair, but I was also careful to avoid traveling in the great Garden State unless by train or plane.

My friend got a kick out of the story as we joked about it, now 15 years later. As I was telling him the details, knowing I'd be driving to see him in New Jersey a few days later for the first time since that ticket, I said quietly to myself, "STOP TALKING ABOUT THIS, MEGAN! You're giving it energy, which could easily make it manifest once more."

The next morning as I was cleaning my house, my thoughts focused on another person, a handsome friend I hadn't seen in awhile. Now this man has a very unique countenance. For starters, he has startling blue eyes with lashes that extend for miles. His sky-high cheekbones accent his thin, long face and together, create an uncommonly attractive visage. I was recalling the last time we got together – a year prior when I first moved into my (dream)home – and I could see his face and feel his presence perfectly. A few hours later, as I was driving through my sleepy little village, I happened to pull into traffic ahead of a cop. When we reached the stoplight on Main Street (two lanes in each direction), my car was at the head of one lane, with the cop I'd pulled in front of about four cars back in the other. I watched as traffic gridlocked itself through that primary intersection, with people breaking all kinds of traffic laws. I found it odd that the cop behind me didn't take any action, not to mention a Sheriff across the intersection who also sat there, ignorant to the ensuing chaos.

"Those turkeys are sleeping on the job!" I (again, snarkily) thought to myself. "They're not paying attention to anything today. I could probably speed my way back home and no one would notice." With that, the light changed and once again we were on our way. At that point, I was only about two streets away from my house, but I needed to change lanes to make the turn. I sped up a little, keeping a loose eye on the cop four cars behind, still thinking, "He's asleep at the wheel and probably wouldn't know if anyone did anything wrong at this point…" I signaled, scooted in front of the lead car, and then slowed down to turn onto my street.

When I was halfway to my house, I saw that the cop was also turning…ONTO MY STREET. At that point, I got a little nervous; cops don't usually drive down my street. Sure enough, just as I was about to turn into my driveway, he put his lights on to pull me over.

"You've got to be FREAKING KIDDING ME!" I said aloud. I pulled into my driveway, stopped the car, and opened the door.

"Please stay in the car," the cop yelled as he stepped out of his vehicle, his lights glaring for all of my neighbors to see. I couldn't imagine what on earth he thought I'd done wrong, so I just grabbed my license and registration and waited for him to approach, one leg hanging out of my opened car door.

"Do you know why I pulled you over?" he said, leaning down so I could see him fully. I couldn't believe it: he looked *identical* to the handsome friend whom I'd been thinking of a few hours prior! He had the *same* piercing blue eyes and impossibly long lashes. The same long, thin face with incredibly high cheekbones. Even the same haircut!

"Uh, not really," I babbled, still in shock about what I was seeing. It even dawned on me that my friend had an identical twin brother, and I had to remind myself that not only did he live six states away, he wasn't even a cop!

"Failure to use your turn signal," he said, taking my license and registration. I waited a few moments while he ran my information, at which point he let me off with a warning. I didn't hear much of what he said, though, still reeling about how I'd manifested such a situation: two thoughts the day before – a New Jersey traffic violation and my handsome friend – funneled into one neat and tidy package! Actually, after the annoyance wore off, I had to smile at the Universe's ingenuity and efficiency. Well played, Universe, well played.

Old & New Friends

A friend who was new to manifesting told me about how he was out one night, hoping to see a friend of his named Katie. "I knew I probably wouldn't see her," he said, admitting that he hadn't seen her in quite some time. "But I *did* end up being approached by another woman named Katie!" I found this interesting from a beginning manifester's standpoint: he affirmed that he wouldn't see the Katie he knew; but her presence in his head nonetheless drew another Katie into his vibratory pull!

Kickball

Interestingly, as that friend was emailing me the Katie story, something else manifested with some kids playing kickball in the yard next to his house. He envisioned the ball flying into his yard and crashing into his window. He saw himself jumping up from the computer, running outside, and yelling at the kids in (what he called) his "current state of undress." Sure enough a few minutes later, he heard the ball crash into his window. He did not, however, run outside naked to reprimand them. ☺

Out to Dinner

One night a friend and I decided to grab a bite to eat together. I suggested a local diner, and immediately envisioned myself eating mashed potatoes (I hadn't had them in awhile and had a real craving!). When we met in the diner's parking lot a bit later, my friend realized that he'd forgotten his shoes. Not his dress-up shoes, mind you, but his *actual* shoes! (This particular friend, during the warmer months, goes barefoot most of the time.)

"Do you think anyone will notice," he said, since neither of us had an extra pair of shoes handy. I did, so we began brainstorming places with outside seating where being shoeless wouldn't be such a big deal.

We ended up at a wood-fired pizzeria with a great outdoor patio. After we ordered our entrees, the waitress brought out some crunchy breadsticks and a cup of what looked like lumpy white butter. Suspicious, we asked her what was in the cup.

"Mashed potatoes!" she said. Shocked – but not necessarily surprised – I laughed and told my friend about my earlier vision of eating mashed potatoes at the diner. His missing shoes had just thrown the Universe a curveball, but it responded anyway – just the way I like my manifesting to go!

Flower Delivery

One Valentine's Day when I was single, I thought how nice it would be if someone sent me flowers. Midway through the morning – and totally out-of-the-blue – one of my boss's vendors emailed me a digitized image of a red rose. It was the first time this particular vendor had ever emailed me for something other than business, and I couldn't have been more delighted.

Traveling Ambitions

A handful of years ago, I remember wanting to travel, but not having any extra money in my budget with which to do so comfortably. Rather than dwell on what I seemingly lacked, I affirmed that I had all the resources I ever needed right at my fingertips, and that travel was easily affordable. Sure enough, within that same week, two things happened.

First, I was asked to edit a friend's book in exchange for airline tickets. Separately, my boss, who owned a condominium in California, suggested I fly out there and stay a few days in order to familiarize myself with his property, agreeing to pay for everything but my food. Off to the west coast!

Message from a Massage Therapist

One night, after seeing a friend post on Facebook about having a massage, I thought to myself, "Wow, that'd be great; I'd love a massage." A few hours later, I received an email from a woman I didn't know. She was a massage therapist who knew a friend of mine, and wanted to get together to talk about manifesting. She was looking for advice and offered to trade a massage for my time.

New Housewares

In my old apartment complex, there was a "flea-market" table in the laundry room. On that table, people left items they no longer wanted and took those left by others. It was a terrific system. One night, I was making mental lists of things I wanted, like a coffee maker and some wine glasses I could use while entertaining. That brought to mind a pair of wine glasses I'd had in my 20's that were gifted to me by a friend. They were hand-painted, but I never used them, so they just sat in a cupboard gathering dust until I placed them on the flea market table a year or so prior.

The morning after thinking about the coffee maker and wine glasses, I walked by the flea-market table; it was full of items from someone who was moving out. Shockingly – although from my perspective as a manifester, not really! – there sat the hand-painted wine glasses I'd given away a year before, not to mention a coffee maker that looked brand new! With a huge smile on my face, I grabbed both and thanked the Universe for answering my call so quickly.

Apartment Hunt

A massage therapist I know needed an apartment. Rather than looking for something traditional, she decided she wanted to live someplace where she could swap massages for rent. She talked to some friends about it, and many were skeptical. Despite these dream-squashers, she held to her vision. Sure enough, while looking through apartment listings on Craigslist one day, there it was: an ad seeking a massage therapist who, in exchange for an apartment, would provide weekly massages to the landlord. Delighted, she moved in shortly thereafter and lived happily with that arrangement for many years.

Boss's Vacation & Dinner Reservations

Since we're always manifesting – whether we consciously direct our thoughts/feelings or not – it doesn't *always* work to our so-called advantage. For example, one week when my boss was on vacation, it dawned on me that even after three days he hadn't reached out to ask me to make any dinner reservations for him. On most of his previous vacations, he gave me a list the first day he was gone and I'd make the plans for his week.

Not even an hour went by after having that thought when suddenly my Blackberry lit up with a new message from my boss. The subject? Dinner reservations. I sort of kicked myself for thinking earlier, "Wow, he hasn't asked me to make reservations this week. Cool!" Instead I probably should have had the thought "Wow, it's been so peaceful with my boss on vacation. I love how much free time I have to focus on the things I want." Lesson learned.

How I Manifested My Dream Home

It was the spring of 2011 and I had decided that rather than continue to live in apartments – which I'd been doing since age ten, when my parents split up – I'd get a house of my own. I guess I'd finally realized that apartment living had become more of a habit than a choice, an assumption based on modeling my behavior after my mother. *She* never got a house when she was single, so why should I? Besides, owning a house is expensive, right? And it's usually reserved for couples, families, or really successful people. While I *did* tell people that I'd buy a house when I found the "right guy," I was happy playing it safe (and small) and staying in my one-bedroom apartment.

The Pocket Guide to Manifesting

Until, of course, I wasn't. Granted, I came to this realization at a time when most people seemed to be selling their homes, downsizing to appease an unpredictable market. Not me. It was time to dream big. So instead of taking the popular conservative route, I decided that the first home I purchased needed to be *spectacular*, not just run-of-the-mill. So I started envisioning myself living amidst multiple bedrooms (for guests!), a beautiful yard, a big porch, and many other things I knew would make me happy.

Despite my grand imaginations, I proceeded with a bit of caution. One of my biggest goals was to make sure I didn't get in over my head, as I was a single woman without a ton of money in the bank. So, I set my desired (and comfortable) price range and found a real estate agent. The first few houses I viewed helped define what I *didn't* want (a lot of immediate maintenance, a crummy or noisy neighborhood, fewer than two bedrooms, a blasé interior…). After three months of looking and one failed offer (mind you, on a house that would have needed major renovations), I grew frustrated. I began thinking, "I'll never find a house I like in my price range."

That's when a friend suggested building a house. I was biased against it, but he assured me I could get something closer to what I wanted if I could find affordable land. So I started looking, and discovered that, indeed, there were unique manufactured housing designs out there. I even fell in love with a particular post-and-beam design, but the price was double what I wanted to pay. Rather than give up, however, I followed a prompt (aka, gut instinct) to revamp the "home" part of a vision board I'd created for just this manifestation.

See, for years I had pictures on my vision board of a Victorian house next to the ocean, with a sweeping side porch, beautiful views, great gardens, and more. Trouble was, that dream was hatched when I was in college a dozen years prior, and was shared by my then-boyfriend, whom I thought I'd marry.

After we split up, I held onto the dream, even though I had evolved well past the person I was when I created that particular housing vision. At one point, I took down the picture of the Victorian house and replaced it with a more sustainable 800-square foot house. I left the picture of the ocean, huge yard, and gardens, though.

That's when I realized that the images were limiting me in terms of manifesting, because in my case I can fall in love with many different styles of something, so long as it has the features I really like. With that in mind, I started from scratch on the housing portion of my vision board, throwing out everything and replacing it with a collage of words and just one image: the post-and-beam house that had recently inspired me. The difference in using that image over the previous ones was that I wasn't married to the style the image represented. Instead, I let myself be excited by the *features* its unique design included: brightness, spaciousness, lots of natural light, maintenance-free, well-

The Pocket Guide to Manifesting

constructed, great location, yard, landscaping, etc. I included the type of feelings I wanted the home to inspire – peaceful, healthy envy, ease, joy, etc. – and then added the key component: easily affordable by me.

Within two weeks of creating my new "dream home" vision board, a house that had been on the market for a couple months fell into my price range. It was a lot of house for the money, and interested parties were urged to act fast because "it wouldn't last long at this price." Well, the price wasn't that low. In fact, it was much more than I wanted to pay, but I thought that if it was meant to be, I could negotiate down into my comfort zone.

So I made an appointment to view it.

It was love at first sight. The moment I walked into the house, I realized it was the style I'd wanted to live in since I was a child: a big old colonial with lots of rooms and a huge front porch. What's more, the interior had been completely renovated two years prior, making it move-in ready. My real estate agent, who had never seen or heard of my vision board, of course, even used some of my words to describe the house. "It's so bright and airy..." Of course I took notice!

Still, enamored as I was walking through each room a few times, fear crept in. This big, beautiful house – the house of my dreams – was simply "too much" house, more than I could handle on my own. As my real estate agent and I stepped out onto the porch and prepared to leave, I was feeling a bit deflated. I absolutely loved the house, but in my current situation – single, planning to live without roommates – I was afraid of high utility bills, barely being able to cover the mortgage, lots of yard work and exterior maintenance, and more. At that moment, a cat from across the street sauntered over and walked directly up to me! I rather like cats, so I bent down to pet it. This felt nice, despite my disappointment about the house. It also – although I couldn't have known it at the time – turned out to be pretty important. But I'll get to that in a minute.

I called my friend, Joy, right away and when she didn't pick up, left a message telling her that I'd just seen my real-life dream house. I described the bedrooms, front porch, great yard, and location. "I love it!" I said. "I think it's too much for me. Maybe with someone else to help with maintenance, utilities, etc. But not on my own. It's just so big and beautiful, though, so I wanted to tell you about it. I'll talk to you later."

I never did speak with Joy that night. I did, however, speak with another friend who lived in Berkeley, California at the time. He listened as I tenderly described the house, my feelings, and my subsequent fear and disappointment that it might be "too much." Funnily, he asked how many square feet it was and the asking price, which I told him. He almost dropped the phone as he shouted, "OH MY GOD! It's *that* big, and it only costs *that* much? Do you have any idea what a house that size would cost in Berkeley? Holy

The Pocket Guide to Manifesting

crap, Megan, you have to buy this house or else I'll buy it and find a way to move it here so I can sell it for a million dollars! Can you buy it and just rent it for a year and live off that money until you're ready to move in?"

His inquiries and enthusiasm made me smile. Sure enough, I was aware of how much house it was for the money, and his energy must have bolstered my own in some respects. After we hung up, I found myself asking the Universe for a sign. "Universe, if I'm meant to make an offer on this house, can you please give me a really clear sign?"

I went to bed that night and dreamt solely of the house.

The next morning, one of the first emails I read was from Mike Dooley's daily inspirational *Notes From the Universe*:

It's kind of strange, Megan, but first you have to know what you want, defined in terms of the end result. And then you have to physically move towards it, without defining the hows. At which point, the thing you want actually starts coming to you, on its own terms, from a direction completely unexpected. Not unlike a cat...

NOT UNLIKE A CAT?! Well, that sure seemed like a sign to me. Still, despite the fact that I would have urged anyone in my situation to run, not walk, to the bank to get a cashiers' check to buy that house on the spot, I was ready to dismiss the whole thing. Fear is *that* powerful sometimes.

The next thing I read was a text on my phone from Joy. "Buy this house!" it started, then went on to share that the love she heard in my voice on my message the night before indicated that my heart *really* wanted it. "If fear is the only thing standing in your way, you should face it," she wrote. "Dream big and let the Universe fill in the spaces of that house with laughter, friends, love – all the stuff you've ever wanted." I kept her text message prominently displayed on my phone most of the day.

I also decided to inquire about the cost of utilities for the property. After receiving the 12-month average, I emailed my agent and asked if we could meet and put together an offer. Sitting in her office a little bit later, I had a number in my mind that was $10,000 less than the newly reduced asking price. My agent had already indicated, while we were touring the house, that I'd be "lucky to get this house for three thousand dollars below the asking price." Not one to heed the well-meaning advice of others if it flies in the face of my manifestations, I dismissed her. So we submitted my first offer. I wanted it to be accepted on-the-spot, and texted a friend to send energy to that effect.

Two hours later, my agent called me: the owner's counter offer was four thousand dollars below their asking price. Unfortunately, this wasn't enough to make that house easily affordable. Did I *really* want to increase my original offer? Could I make that work financially over time? (Fear, fear, and more fear!)

I decided to sleep on it. The next morning, I got an email from the friend I'd asked to send energy about my first offer. He told me that my approach felt too controlling to him, and that I should just let it play out how it would. This reminded me of one of the manifesting rules: focus on the end result. Trying to control the details was just a "how" in disguise. So I realigned myself with what mattered – that the process be easy and that the house stay easily affordable. I admitted that while my initial offer was definitely in my comfort zone, it wasn't my ceiling; two thousand dollars more would be my ceiling. So I had a decision to make: counter back or let the house go. Two thousand seemed like a lot of money. Or was it?

I thought about it all morning, at one point asking for another clear sign from the Universe: should I counter that offer or not? I reached out to a handful of friends who had been supporting me throughout the process. One of them responded with stunning clarity:

"What's a couple thousand MEAN? Not 'how much is it?' What is your *dream* worth?"

That last line got me. He was absolutely right. What was my *dream* worth? Certainly another two thousand dollars! What's more, if I could see two thousand dollars as being chump change (!) and not quibble over it, then that energy would attach itself to my counter offer and the owners of the house wouldn't quibble over sacrificing another four thousand dollars, either. I submitted my counter offer, and then called my friend, Joy, again.

Early on in the conversation, Joy was telling me how much she loved to paint rooms in houses. "Ohhhhh, that could be good," I thought. "I'm going to have some rooms that need touching up."

"Okay, Megan," said Joy as the conversation was winding up. "So I'm manifesting that you're just going to call me later today and tell me that you got the house! I mean, that's something you'd call me about, right?"

"Of course I'd call you!" I said. "You'll be one of the first people I call."

"Good, because then after you tell me you got the house, I'm going to tell you that I'm getting a ticket to New York to come visit!"

"Oh my gosh, that would be fantastic. I would love that!"

"Okay, great. Now I have *no idea* how I'm going to manifest a ticket to New York, but I figure if you can manifest your dream home, I can manifest a plane ticket!"

After we hung up, I concocted another manifestation in which I envisioned my agent calling a short while later and saying something like, "I don't know what you did, but they accepted. Congratulations!"

After spending a few seconds with that manifestation, I let it go. "Whatever happens, happens," I told myself. I deleted all the texts I'd gotten about the house from supportive friends, looked at a few other ads for houses online, and then, secure that I'd released all desire for a preferred outcome with this particular house, decided to take a nap. I slept soundly for the next two hours with the phone turned off.

The Pocket Guide to Manifesting

When I awoke I had a voicemail message from my agent. "Well, Megan, your good vibes must have worked because you have a signed counter offer. Congratulations!"

I stumbled from my bedroom into the hallway, trying to shake sleep from me.

Oh... My... GOD! I thought as I rubbed my eyes, and then caught a glimpse of myself in the mirror; I was smiling.

I started saying aloud, "Oh my god! OH MY GOD!!! Thank you, Universe, thank you!"

The next thing I knew I was excitedly dialing Joy's number. I thought, "Come onnnnn... Pick up, pick up, pick up."

"Hello?" she said.

"Joy? I GOT THE HOUSE! I GOT THE HOUSE! I GOT THE HOUSE!" I was laughing and sort of jumping up and down while telling her.

"Oh my God, Megan, you got it?" She was laughing whole-heartedly. "Wow! You're going to be a homeowner. I've got to get a ticket to New York!"

We spent the next five minutes laughing together and excitedly talking about how it all came together, marveling about how my ability to envision end results truly resulted in manifesting such magic! Not long after, Joy flew to New York and we relived the story all over again – while sipping tea on my beautiful front porch, that is!

APPENDIX 2:
My Manifestation Worksheet

1. What is it I am wanting to manifest?

2. Is this really what I want to manifest? If not, can I be more specific? (Refer to pages 19-21 for guidance.)

3. What are the feelings I am going to feel once I've manifested what I want*?

4. With these feelings in mind, can I step into a space right now of feeling as if I already have the thing I want? (Remember: the stronger the feeling, the more strongly I magnetize.)

5. Which tools will I use to help keep me positively focused on this thing that I want?

    a. Vision Boards/Word Collages
    b. Affirmations (such as, "I have everything I want and need in abundant supply! I am a manifesting master! This stuff is easy!")
    c. Gratitude Exercises ("I am so grateful that I now have what I want. My life feels amazing to me. Thank you, Universe, thank you!")
    d. Mirror Writing

e. Phone Reminders (a good place to put affirmations and gratitude phrases)

   f. Feng Shui and/or Intention Setting

   g. Creative Renaming

   h. Media-Inspired Visions such as inspirational TV Shows/Web Sites/Movies/Songs

6. Would any of these phrases benefit me in terms of how I've worded my desire?

   a. In a good and balanced way

   b. Best yet

   c. Beyond my fondest dreams

   d. Easily affordable by me

7. What small action can I take right now that would put me out there in life where the Universe can meet me?

8. Am I remembering that everything is possible and that the things I want also want me? Can I remind myself of that if I feel any resistance to this process?

9. Am I remembering that manifesting is fun and is something I can do any time?

---

* Possible feelings: excitement, elation, relief, amazement, bliss...etc.

ACKNOWLEDGEMENTS

My heartfelt thanks to:

Joy, for inciting me to write this book.
Sue, for making it look pretty.
Chris, for editing me.
Kristen, for focusing me.
Mary Beth, for artifying me.
Steve, for teaching me.
Tess, for inspiring me.
Vic, for best-friending me.
My family and friends, for loving and encouraging me.
Jim, for romancing me (…beyond my fondest dreams!).

And of course, to the Universe, for being an eternal ocean of magic and miracles, which continuously invites us all to dive in!

Thank you, thank you, thank you!